The Israeli Dilemma

The Israeli Dilemma

A debate between two left-wing Jews

Letters between
Marcel Liebman and Ralph Miliband

Selected, with an introduction and epilogue
by Gilbert Achcar

Translated from the French by Peter Drucker

MERLIN PRESS

First published in the UK 2006
by The Merlin Press Ltd.
96 Monnow Street
Monmouth
NP25 3EQ
Wales
www.merlinpress.co.uk

ISBN. 0850365767

British Library Cataloguing in Publication Data

Printed in the UK by MPG Books Ltd., Bodmin, Cornwall

Contents

Acknowledgements

This work is being published under the auspices of the Marcel Liebman Foundation of Brussels, which is run by Mateo Alaluf, Henri Hurwitz and Nicole Mayer. Daniel Liebman, Marcel Liebman' s nephew, has made a major contribution to it. Daniel and I selected the letters jointly from the Foundation's collection, and Daniel entered them onto the computer. He has supplied me with texts, documents and information without which my own contribution to this work would not have been possible. Thanks to Peter Drucker for his translation and comments, and to Stephen Shalom for his reading and suggestions.

Gilbert Achcar

Introduction

About Israel: from a friendly disagreement…
by Gilbert Achcar

In the first half of 1967 the situation in the Middle East had worsened. There were sharp tensions between Syria and Israel, exchanges of artillery fire, and an Israeli air raid. Israel had called on Syria to put an end to incursions by Palestinian fedayeen from Syrian territory, and rejected a Syrian offer of a ceasefire. On 13 May Moscow informed Egypt that Israel was massing troops along its frontier with Syria.

Cairo sent troops into the Sinai to show its solidarity with Syria and then, in order to make its deterrent threat credible, asked to have the UN forces withdrawn that had been stationed along the Israeli-Egyptian frontier since 1956.[1] Then on 22 May, Cairo declared it was closing the Gulf of Aqaba to Israeli shipping or any strategic cargo bound for the Israeli port of Eilat.

At the beginning of June a government of national unity was formed in Israel. This was the prelude to the attack launched in the early morning of 5 June 1967, the beginning of the so-called Six-Day War. In the course of this war Israel seized the West Bank from Jordan, the Gaza Strip and the whole Sinai from Egypt and the Golan Heights from Syria.

---

1   The blue-helmeted troops of the United Nations Emergency Force had been stationed only on the Egyptian side of the frontier, since Israel had refused to allow them on its territory since UNEF's creation in 1956.

The following correspondence begins with a letter dated 28 May 1967, sent by Ralph Miliband (1924-1994) to Marcel Liebman (1929-1986), his closest friend. These two brilliant intellectuals[2] had very many things in common. Both had been born in Brussels to Polish Jewish immigrant parents; both had been deeply affected by the experience of Nazism and the Second World War. They had become friends in London in 1953, when Liebman was studying international relations at the London School of Economics (LSE), where Miliband was teaching. They shared the same Marxist perspective while maintaining their independence from party apparatuses, which the two of them were equally suspicious of. Less than this has often been enough to found a strong 'elective affinity'; and in fact these two men's friendship proved solid enough to withstand any of the tests it was put to.

This exchange of letters was one such test, and a particularly difficult one, for the question of Israel was the most serious stumbling block that the deep intellectual partnership between Miliband and Liebman ever ran up against. It may seem paradoxical that two Jews, both of whose lives were intensely affected by the trauma of the destruction of the European Jews, linked by their shared political thought, came into conflict over (of all things) the attitude they should adopt towards a state that defined itself as 'Jewish' and claimed a legitimacy founded on the centuries-old oppression of the Jews. Yet to think this would be to forget that both of them, as Marxists or people much inclined towards Marxism, were at bottom internationalists. Both refused to be trapped in any identity whatsoever that would predetermine their attitudes; both were hostile to any kind of nationalist narrow-mindedness.

---

2   The two authors' best-known works are Ralph Miliband, *The State in Capitalist Society: The Analysis of the Western System of Power*, London: Weidenfeld & Nicolson, 1969 (many later editions); Marcel Liebman, *Leninism under Lenin*, London: Merlin Press, 1980 (originally published as *Le léninisme sous Lénine*, Paris: Editions du Seuil, 1973).

The paradox lies elsewhere, and is a rather common one all in all in the vast range of positions taken on the question of Israel. It consists in the fact that the more intransigent of the two friends in his attitude towards the state of Israel, was at the same time the one who was more saturated in Jewish religious culture because of his family background, as well as the one whose experience of the long night of Nazism had been the most tragic: Marcel Liebman had experienced the everyday terror of the German occupation of Belgium; his older brother Henri had been deported to Auschwitz and died there.[3] Marcel told the story of this terrible experience of his youth in an admirable autobiographical work, containing both valuable testimony and deep-going reflection, which has still not had the success it deserves beyond his native Belgium. Its title is *Born Jewish*.[4]

The book ends with a remarkable chapter in which he draws up a balance sheet of his Jewishness and his intellectual and political commitment:

I had gradually set myself apart from the Jewish community, doing so without either passion or acrimony: a detachment rather than a rejection. My path took me towards new allegiances which now gave me a closeness to comrades rather than co-religionists. As for my religious faith, it did not shatter; it withered and well and truly died: slow death throes which spared me any suffering. My Jewishness itself was on the way to becoming unspoken, then I was brought back to it through the round-about route of politics.[...]

So the Algerian war was my first encounter with the Arab-Jewish problem. It led me, without my having wished for it, into involvement in political actions as a Jew, even though my deep motivation had nothing to do with this particular consideration

---

3   Ralph Miliband had the good fortune to be able to leave Belgium with his father for Britain, where he joined the navy in 1943. See his biography by Michael Newman, *Ralph Miliband and the Politics of the New Left*, London: Merlin Press, 2002.

4   Marcel Liebman, *Born Jewish: a Childhood in Occupied Europe*, translated by Liz Heron and introduced by Jacqueline Rose, London: Verso, 2005.

and was rooted in my anti-colonialist convictions.
Experience showed me the damage wrought by the anti-
Arab racism of some Jews. Appalled, I had also observed the
development of an unconditional pro-Israeli stance that paralysed
a great many Jews, even the progressives, over the question of
distancing themselves from Zionist policies.[5]

'As a Jew': Marcel Liebman rediscovered his own Jewishness as
a reaction against recurrent attempts to equate Jewishness on the
one hand with hostility towards Arabs and support to the Israeli
state's policies on the other — in order to deny others the right to
establish themselves as the Jews' exclusive representatives.[6] He was
nonetheless far removed from 'that all-too notorious *jüdischer
Selbsthass*, that "Jewish self-hatred" that is the imbeciles' eternal
argument against any Jew who strays even slightly from the beaten
path of the tribe', as Pierre Vidal-Naquet wrote vigorously in his
posthumous tribute to Marcel Liebman.[7] Vidal-Naquet cited on
this subject the admirable lines that Liebman had written in 1973

5 Ibid., pp. 169-70.
6 The same causes still lead to the same effects. Thus in France many years later
a group of intellectuals of Jewish ancestry felt the need to distance themselves
from the same, resurgent tendency — 'as Jews'. Their manifesto, published
under this title in the newspaper *Le Monde* on 19 October 2000, declared: 'As
citizens of the country in which we live and citizens of the planet, we neither
see reasons for, nor are in the habit of, expressing ourselves as Jews.... But the
rulers of the state of Israel, by claiming to speak in the name of all the world's
Jews, appropriating collective Jewish memory, and appointing themselves
representatives of all past Jewish victims, are also usurping the right to speak
in our name over our objections. Nobody has a monopoly of the Nazi genocide
of the Jews. Our families too have had their share of deportees, disappeared
and resistance fighters. Blackmail on the grounds of community solidarity, in
order to legitimate the politics of national unity of Israeli governments, is also
intolerable to us.... It is not in spite of being Jewish but rather because we are
Jewish that we oppose this suicidal logic of identity-based panic. We reject the
deadly spiral of ethnicization of the conflict and its transformation into a war of
religions. We refuse to be nailed to the wall of communal identity.'
7 Pierre Vidal-Naquet, 'Pour un ami disparu: Hommage à Marcel Liebman',
published initially in *Revue d'Etudes Palestiniennes* (Paris), no. 30, Winter 1989,
then republished in Vidal-Naquet, *Les Juifs, la mémoire et le présent* (2nd ed.),
Paris: La Découverte, 1991. This citation is from the following edition, Paris:
Points, 1995, p. 496.

and that Vidal-Naquet fully identified with:

> The long trail of horror and suffering that marks the passage of human history and lines up the Treblinka's and Auschwitz's as it passes by does not lead to the *kibbutzim,* military or not, but rather to the concentration camps where the Palestinian people is vegetating and dying, plundered and negated by the Israelis and by the auxiliaries that Israelis have found in the Arab camp. And if it must be said briefly: some Jews declare their solidarity with the Palestinians, not in spite of their own origin, but *because* of their origin and a certain logic that their origin induces in their view. This logic leads them, almost by definition, to take the side of the oppressed: in this case the Palestinians, the Jews of the Middle East. [8]

Like many left-wing opponents of Zionism, Marcel Liebman rejected the pessimistic postulate, which has served as the foundation for the principle that Jews must be assembled in a single 'Jewish state', that anti-Semitism is ineluctable or even natural. His attitude was part of his overarching rejection of any assertion of the inevitability of racism in general, which more often than not is aimed at rendering commonplace or justifying a particular brand of racism. Not that Marcel was a starry-eyed believer in the natural, spontaneous improvement of the human race; on the contrary, his beliefs all bore the stamp of political realism and militant resolution. He had made of the anti-racist struggle a categorical imperative, anchored in a sense of moral debt to his own martyred brother Henri.

> Shall I be taxed with dangerous optimism because I do not believe in the inevitability of racism in general and of anti-Jewish hatred in particular? What I do believe is that these scourges will not disappear naturally but need to be fought against actively. The vicissitudes of this struggle may justify exile in certain circumstances. But the systematic exodus that Zionism advocates

seems to me to offer no solution: it uproots, it maims, and it leaves the field to the enemy.

Yes, to the enemy. Any obligation I have felt to the dead of the war and, if one wished to personalise this, to one of them in particular, is a duty that comes down to this: holding the racism that murdered them to be a crime in which no one ever colludes.[9]

Ralph Miliband for his part, according to his biographer,

was vehemently opposed to any suggestion that Jewishness defined his *primary* identity, and after 1945 he had been determined that his life would not be conditioned and constrained by consciousness of the Nazi Holocaust or anti-Semitism more generally. Instead he insisted that his commitment to socialism constituted his primary identity, and he always aspired to define a *socialist* position on key events and strategic decisions. [10]

In the early 1960s he had drafted notes whose title, 'On Being a Non-Jewish Jew', referred to the famous lecture given by Isaac Deutscher in 1958, which was later published in a collection bearing the same title.[11] In his notes Ralph Miliband opposed two ways of being Jewish.

I do *not* reject [and] cannot reject a low level kind of Jewish iden-tity; birth, family background, culture, Yiddish, etc. Find it quite compatible with any other type of commitment [...] *But* I am asked to believe that *beyond* all such allegiances I have a bond with Jews as Jews. [...]

I reject this, for [the] simple reason that I belong to a 'party', of people whom I recognise as *my* party, my people, be they French, English, German, Jew, Gentile, black, yellow or what. [...] I have

9 Liebman, *Born Jewish*, pp. 180.
10 Newman, op.cit., pp. 126-27.
11 Isaac Deutscher, *The Non-Jewish Jew and Other Essays*, London: Oxford University Press, 1968.

more in common with my kind of socialist goy than with a conservative, reactionary or what sort of Jew. [...]

Socialism does not exclude *my* kind of Jewishness. But [it] excludes [the] racist all-goys-are-enemies kind.[12]

Nevertheless, despite their fundamentally common view, Miliband's relationship to his Jewishness was less tormented than Liebman's. He experienced his break with identity-based tribalism as something much less anguished, in a British context that made it less fraught.[13] Inversely, Marcel Liebman's instinctive reaction against the unconditional loyalty to Israel that was very much present in his Belgian and French environment clearly bolstered his anti-Zionist intransigence.

Ralph was convinced that Marcel pushed his anti-Zionism to extremes, not in spite of being Jewish but rather because of being Jewish. This explains his comical challenge to Marcel in his first letter, written at a moment when tensions were dangerously on the rise on the Israeli-Arab front. Ralph appeals to his friend not to bend the stick too far, with a humorous reference to the internationalism they share: 'Being Jewish does not in itself justify a frenzied pro-Arab attitude.'

Marcel took the witticism poorly, perhaps because it rubbed the sore place of his uneasy Jewishness. We get a glimpse of this when, after having passionately defended his radically anti-Zionist point of view in his torrent of a letter on 30-31 May and having reproached Ralph with reacting as 'a Jew rather than as a socialist', he heaves this concluding sigh: 'And yet God knows that I feel Jewish in all sorts of ways.'

Challenged in turn, Ralph searches his conscience in his

---

12   Michael Newman generously provided me with a copy of these notes. The originals are in the Ralph Miliband archives deposited in the Leeds University Library.

13   In his notes for a lecture on the concept of the 'non-Jewish Jew' as Isaac Deutscher defined it, a lecture delivered to the LSE Jewish Society on 3 December 1969, Ralph Miliband began by clarifying that he had 'no particular expertise', 'unlike Deutscher, who was steeped in Jewish tradition, both religious and secular' (notes provided by Michael Newman).

response on 2 June. He makes an effort to be as honest as possible, acknowledging that 'an emotional element enters into play' in his refusal to envisage the elimination of the state of Israel preached by the Arab side.[14]

> And yet I hope with all my heart and mind that it isn't as a Jew that I would find this awful, *but as a socialist*, that is, as someone who is bound to seek human measurements in order to judge historical events.

The dilemma that much of the Western left — not only left-wing Jews, far from it — faced with the outbreak of the June 1967 war was a very painful one: the tension between their left-wing convictions and the 'emotional element', a tension that incidentally persists until this day. The spirit of the time in 1967 was still very much infused on the left with a vigorous anti-colonialism, and for the most radical leftists with anti-imperialism. For many left-wing Jews the dilemma really did correspond to the one that Albert Camus had pronounced his judgment on ten years earlier in Stockholm when he declared that he would choose defending his mother above justice. For non-Jews the emotional factor was admittedly less acute, but it was no less serious. It took the specific form of keen feelings of guilt about genocidal Nazi anti-Semitism and the forms of active and passive complicity with Nazism that had existed in the West.

Jean-Paul Sartre, whose tormented attitude towards the Jewish question and exemplary struggle against imperialism are both well known, was tailor-made to express this dilemma. In his preface to the voluminous special issue that *Les Temps Modernes* devoted in 1967 to the Israeli-Arab conflict, after having referred to the extermination of the Jews, Sartre added:

---

14   Newman (op. cit., p. 135) implies that Miliband was responding to the influence of his wife, Marion Kozak-Miliband, whose mother was living in Israel and who for this reason was concerned about Israel's security. But Marion challenges this interpretation. She insists that Ralph's attitude was due fundamentally to the fact that he considered the prospect of the destruction of the Israeli nation-state humanly reprehensible,

I simply wished to recall that for many of us an emotional
determination exists that is not for all that a characteristic of
our subjectivity without particular importance, but is rather
a general effect of historical, perfectly objective circumstances
that we are nowhere near forgetting. […] Thus we find within
ourselves rigorous and contradictory exigencies — *our* exigencies:
'Imperialism forms a whole that must be fought everywhere and in
all its forms, in Vietnam, Venezuela, Santo Domingo, Greece and
also in all its efforts to establish its power in the Middle East' —
and 'The idea of the Arabs' destroying the Jewish state and driving
its citizens into the sea cannot be tolerated for a moment, unless I
am a racist.' Torn apart, we do not dare to do or say anything…[15]

The fact is that in 1967, even after the Israeli armed forces'
lightning, crushing and simultaneous victory in June over three
Arab countries' armies, the idea of a danger of extermination
hanging over the state of Israel was still very much alive. The self-
deluding threats of Arab nationalist vociferation — personified
by Ahmed Shukeiry, chairman of the Palestine Liberation
Organization until Yassir Arafat's movement took control of it
beginning in 1968 — kept an anxiety alive that Israeli leaders
exploited ably in order to galvanize their own population and
ensure themselves of very broad international support.

Peter Novick, in his excellent book on the use of the Holocaust
in collective memory, has described this moment very well, in
terms that can just as well be applied to European Jews:

As is well known, the spring of 1967 was a dramatic turning point
in American Jews' relationship to Israel. […] The great majority
of American Jews, including many who had not previously shown
the slightest interest in Israel, were in a state of high anxiety, and
plunged into a flurry of rallies and fund-raising. In fact, Israel
was hardly in serious peril. Shortly before the outbreak of war
in June, President Lyndon Johnson's intelligence experts debated

---

independently of the injustice on which this state had been founded (e-
mail from Marion Kozak-Miliband to Gilbert Achcar).

15 Jean-Paul Sartre, 'Pour la vérité', preface to the dossier *Le conflit israélo-
arabe* in the journal *Les Temps Modernes*, no. 253 bis, 1967, pp. 10-11.

whether it would take a week or ten days for Israel to demolish its enemies. But this was not the understanding of American Jews, for whom Israel was poised on the brink of destruction — and it is our perceptions of reality, not the reality itself, that shape our responses.[16]

One has to remember this context in order to understand the admiration that Ralph Miliband felt, despite their disagreements, for the bravura with which his friend publicly expressed his radically anti-Zionist views in 1967 — at the price of deeply wounding insults and even death threats, proffered by people for whom any Jew who criticizes Israel is a 'traitor'. 'One can never sufficiently praise the courage and determination that Marcel and his wife Adeline showed', wrote Ralph in his eulogy for Marcel about his friend's attitude in 1967.[17]

One must also keep this same context in mind in order not to misinterpret Ralph Miliband's attitude. The letters in which he expresses the greatest concern about the Zionist state's fate are the ones written before 5 June 1967. After the Six-Day War the drastic turnaround in Israel's image, from potential victim to 'an elite people, sure of themselves and domineering', to borrow General de Gaulle's resounding formula,[18] shook Ralph's attitude considerably. This no doubt explains his long delay in responding to Marcel's letter dated 5 June 1967, the day the war began. The various draft letters, dated 7, 16 and 26 June, bear witness to Ralph's hesitation before the letter that he would ultimately send on 2 July.

In his draft of 16 June 1967 — the only one of the three included in this collection, so as to trace the evolution of his thinking while

16   Peter Novick, *The Holocaust in American Life*, Boston: Houghton Mifflin, 1999, p. 148. The title of the British edition was changed to *The Holocaust and Collective Memory: The American Experience*, in order to emphasize the more general meaning of its analyses. Reading this book is urgently to be recommended today, as tensions around the issue of anti-Semitism are again on the rise.

17   Miliband, 'Un itinéraire intellectuel', in *Marcel Liebman*, special issue of *Points Critiques*, quarterly review of the Union of Progressive Jews of Belgium (Brussels), no. 25, May 1986, p. 11.

18   From de Gaulle's press conference on 27 November 1967. The French

avoiding the inevitable repetitions — he acknowledges, 'My silence has been due to the fact that I've been thinking over our correspondence in light of recent events, and been trying to judge to what extent they undermine my views and confirm yours.' Then he admits to being 'frankly torn apart by contradictory considerations' on the subject of the war that had just taken place.

But until the end, nevertheless, while much more inclined after the Six-Day War to criticize the Zionist state, Ralph Miliband remains strongly attached to what he considered the central point of their discussion, and underscores as such in his letter of 2 July: the necessity of accepting the existence of the state of Israel. Marcel Liebman for his part, as his response on 4 July shows, also moderates his own position, probably influenced by the discussions and actions after Israel's lightning victory that he had got involved in.

We can mention in particular the manifesto entitled 'For a solution of the Israeli-Arab conflict' that he had drafted and published on 9 June 1967 together with many prominent Belgians, including 14 MPs and senators, many of his colleagues at the Free University of Brussels, lawyers, journalists, trade unionists and well-known activists of the Communist and Trotskyist left — including many people of Jewish origin like

---

president's choice of words provoked considerable indignation — rightly, since he was referring not to Israel but to Jews in general — 'at all times', to top it off! As a reminder, here is the citation in context: 'The establishment between the two world wars — since we must go that far back — of a Zionist homeland in Palestine and then, after the Second World War, the establishment of the State of Israel gave rise at the time to a certain number of apprehensions. The question could be asked, and was indeed asked even among many Jews, whether the settlement of this community on lands acquired under more or less justifiable conditions, in the midst of Arab populations who were thoroughly hostile to it, would not lead to incessant, interminable frictions and conflicts. Some people even feared that the Jews, until then dispersed, but who had remained what they had been at all times, that is an elite people, sure of themselves and domineering, would, once assembled again on the site of their ancient greatness, turn the very moving desires that they had been accumulating for nineteen centuries into a burning, conquering ambition.'

him.[19] The intransigence that Marcel had shown in his polemic with his friend Ralph had softened as the demands of realism and consensus, without which political action risks becoming irrational, imposed moderation on him.

The exchange between the two friends, which had begun *appassionato*, ended *moderato*, without ever ceasing to be *affettuoso*.

---

19   See the footnote in Ralph Miliband's letter of 2 July 1967, included in this collection.

Letters of
Marcel Liebman and Ralph Miliband
28 May – 4 July 1967

The following letters were written in French, the language in which Marcel Liebman and Ralph Miliband, both born in Brussels, communicated with each other. Miliband, who had moved to Britain when he was 16, had better English. His letters, and to a lesser extent Marcel Liebman's as well, are studded with English phrases and expressions, printed here in italics. Passages that were underscored in the letters are also underscored here, in keeping with the typed originals.

[*Letterhead: London School of Economics and Political Science*]

28 May 1967

Dear Marcel,

We're really very happy to hear that you're recovering and are able to work, in fact to work very well indeed. This is very good news, and we send our best wishes for a continuing recovery so that you can soon put the whole thing behind you.[1]
[...]

This brings me to the Israeli events. Marion and I have been wondering for some days now what your attitude is: Marion is convinced that you're supporting Nasser completely, while I on the other hand think you're not as sectarian as all that.... *Anyway* I would like to share with you my own views on the subject:

1. Being Jewish does not in itself justify a frenzied pro-Arab attitude.

2. The only basis on which the blockade of the Gulf of Aqaba can be defended is acceptance of the goal of destroying the state of Israel. Once you accept that, there's no problem. If you don't, then I think it's impossible to support a measure that can have no other goal besides weakening Israel's position in a war of annihilation in the more or less near future.

3. On the subject of the destruction of Israel, one may reasonably have doubts about the wisdom of having created the state. But that is a fairly academic question now. The state exists.

---

1   Marcel Liebman had been ill with hepatitis for a month.

The alternative, the elimination of the state — and with it its citizens, since most of them will reject this alternative — does not seem to me a policy that socialists worthy of the name could support.

4. This in no way prevents anyone from condemning the Israelis for their foreign policy, Suez,[2] etc. Let us condemn these policies in the name of socialist principles, but without putting the existence of the state in question. After all I condemn the Americans but don't put their national existence in question. Nor have I ever put the national existence of Germany in question; on the contrary, I've always fought against those who talked about dismembering [Germany], etc. The fact that Israel is a relatively new state doesn't change anything.

5. These basic ideas also depend on the thesis that the existence of Israel is in no way a threat to national or (hypothetical) socialist revolutions in the Arab countries. I have no problem admitting that Israel is a pawn of American imperialism, though the phrase is exaggerated. But I wholly fail to see how Israel is holding back Nasser's revolution in Egypt or anywhere else. The idea is absurd. If we need imperialist candidates then the Shah of Persia, [King] Hussein [of Jordan] and [King] Feisal [of Saudi Arabia] are better ones; but nobody suggests that their countries, which are clearly distinct from them as individuals, should disappear. In fact Israel serves as a <u>pretext</u> for the Arab leaders, including Nasser, who are not much inclined to transform their revolutions, where there are revolutions, in truly socialist ways.

6. Many people on the left, I would say most of them, are prone to be taken in all too quickly by the rhetoric of Arab socialism, although they have become much more sceptical about African socialism. In reality Nasser's claims to socialism leave a lot to be desired. His regime is after all a semi-military, bureaucratic

---

2   A reference to Israel's participation in the Franco-British aggression against Egypt in 1956 following the nationalization of the Suez Canal.

dictatorship, where nationalisations still leave considerable
room for inequality and exploitation and any independent left
is brutally repressed, often with the help of former Gestapo
officials etc. I don't doubt that Nasser plays a <u>positive</u> role in
the Middle East by contributing to the disappearance of feudal
regimes; this is why I support him in that respect. The same goes
for his anti-imperialist and anti-colonial crusades, which are
bit less clear but nonetheless real. All this is really a progressive
factor that the left should support. <u>But this does not mean that
we should support him in all his undertakings, including his
anti-Israeli undertakings,</u> or his anti-communist undertakings
for that matter. The sad thing is that this sterling left is incapable
of distinguishing anything from anything, and reacts with a
truly Pavlovian predictability to the slogans used to make it
drool on cue. I repeat, someone would have to demonstrate
very clearly to me just <u>how</u> Israel is a brake on the Arab socialist
revolution, or rather hinders it, in order to justify the avowed
intention of Nasser etc. to put an end to the state itself. I don't
believe there is any way to demonstrate this.

7. I doubt that you will agree with these propositions. But I
would like you to examine them without starting from the belief
that they are the product of Israeli sentimentalism. It is true
that I would consider the extermination of two million Jews,
including hundreds of thousands of survivors of the camps, as
an appalling catastrophe. But I like to think that I would feel just
the same way if I were not Jewish myself.

8. I find it quite amusing that the world communist left — the
Chinese, the Russians, etc. — should have finally managed to
agree on something: denouncing the Israelis' imperialist threats
and backing Nasser to the bitter end. This support *incidentally*
falls into the category of the most total opportunism, and is the
same kind of reflex that made them support Sukarno and his
national revolution. It is no duty of socialists to support pseudo-
socialist revolutions unconditionally; they should do it in a
nuanced way. But the rottenness of official Marxism in our time

makes this kind of attitude impossible, even leaving aside the role of state interests.

Enough for today, but I wanted you to know my views on a subject that preoccupies us both. Tell me soon what you think about it.

Your friend,

Ralph

[*Letterhead: Clos des Pommiers Fleuris*]

Brussels, 30 May 1967

Dear Ralph and Marion,

Will our friendship survive a clash like this…? I hope it does.
But honesty compels me to say that Marion, armed with her
admirable intuition and unaided by Marxist dialectics, was right.
I've chosen the wrong side again; and without taking entirely
Nasserite or Syrian positions I remain, in this episode of the
Israeli-Arab conflict as in earlier ones, on the Arab side. I wanted
to write to both of you on this subject this very morning. But
I told myself that trying to explain my position would require
so much of me… Now, faced with the provocation of Ralph's
letter, I no longer have any choice. I've pulled page 257 of *La
Révolution Russe*[3] out of my typewriter and rolled in page 1 of
my pro-Arab brief. Nevertheless I claim the right to be almost as
schematic as Ralph was in his letter. But I have also been telling
myself in the last few days that it would not be a bad thing for
the [*Socialist*] *Register* to tackle this thorny problem in its pages
— not, I reassure you, that this means I am putting myself
forward for the task.[4]

1) Preliminary remark: you [Ralph] question the weakness
that the left has in your eyes for Arab socialism. You say that
'this sterling left is incapable of distinguishing anything from

---

3   Later published in English as *The Russian Revolution: The Origins, Phases
     and Meaning of the Bolshevik Victory*, trans. by Arnold J. Pomerans with a
     preface by Isaac Deutscher, London: Cape, 1970.
4   The *Socialist Register* published an article by Marcel Liebman on 'Israel,
     Palestine and Zionism' in its 1970 issue (Ralph Miliband and John Saville
     eds., London: Merlin Press, 1970).

anything, and reacts with a truly Pavlovian predictability to
the slogans used to make it drool on cue'. I suppose we must be
living on two different planets, and that the *Channel* makes a
world of difference. I in fact am just as willing as you are to heap
sarcastic abuse on the left, but for completely opposite reasons.
If I am to judge by what is happening in Belgium — but leave
Belgium aside, it doesn't matter much — and France, the left
is entirely on the side of Israel. Yes, it swallows slogans whole
and gobbles up clichés. But its blindness and sentimentalism
are all to Israel's benefit. Let's put the Communists aside for
the moment. Except for a few very very very rare exceptions,
the whole French left is basically for Israel. There is a Zionist
front running from Sartre to Guy Mollet.[5] If it's different in
England, if the Edelmans, Orbachs and other Zionist-Labourites
are the exception, then this only increases my desire to move
to your country. In any case, outside England, the myth we
have to fight against — but by what means, I ask you? (but I'm
thinking about it just the same and will try to do it in the next
few days, at the risk of being called every name you can imagine,
including traitor, anti-Semite, victim of *jüdischer Selbsthass*[6] and
other idiocies) — is the myth of Israel as a peaceful, progressive,
democratic, quasi-socialist islet that must be defended at all
costs against the fanatical, destructive Arabs following in Hitler's
footsteps and so on and so forth. Of course I'm not claiming
that you have succumbed to this myth. I'm saying that this is
the myth, this and nothing else. If the (French) Communists
have avoided this pitfall and not fallen into the trap of Israeli
propaganda and pro-Jewish sentimentalism, it's their lockstep
loyalty to the USSR and nothing else that has protected them.
For once in a rare while it turns out to be fortunate.

---

5   Leader of the French social democratic party SFIO under whose
     government the French took part in the tripartite attack on Egypt in
     1956.
6   'Jewish self-hatred' (in German).

The myth of Arab socialism is *irrelevant* here. We may have
different opinions on what Nasserism amounts to. But doubtless
there would only be nuances of difference between us. To cite
one passage from your letter: 'Nasser plays a positive role in
the Middle East by contributing to the disappearance of feudal
regimes... The same goes for his anti-imperialist and anti-
colonial crusades...' So here there's nothing for us to discuss:
I agree with you on this point, just as I agree with all the
criticisms you make of Nasser. So let's not clog up the discussion
with an Arab myth that neither one of us believes in. And the
Communists obviously don't believe in it any more than we do,
even though they support Nasser and Syria and are right to do
so. (Between you and me, the Syrian case is more interesting
right now than Egypt. Syria's leftwards shift strikes me as more
convincing — but you'll say that after the illusions I had about
Algeria I'd be better off being cautious. OK, OK...). And let's
not weigh down the discussion with phrases like, 'Being Jewish
does not in itself justify a frenzied pro-Arab attitude.'

2) There are three ways of viewing the current crisis, and
the three levels are of course not entirely separable from
one another: the international context; its specific unfolding
(meaning the events of the last fortnight); and the most
fundamental level, the Israeli problem as a whole. I will deal
with these two last aspects. On the most recent developments I
have 4 observations to make:

a) Let us imagine that the cause of everything is the Arab raids.
So be it. Curiously, during the months of April and May there
were, according to the Israelis, 13 raids from either Syria or
Lebanon and 8 from Jordan. What is strange and significant is
that Israel is only threatening Syria. And in what way? This is
what General [Yitzhak] Rabin, the Israeli military chief of staff,
proclaimed on 14 May: 'As long as the revolutionary blowhards
in Damascus have not been overthrown, no government in the
Middle East can feel secure.' I don't know if Israel was preparing
to attack Syria, as the Arabs and Soviets claim, whether or not in

cahoots with the CIA. But what is certain is that there had been a series of verbal threats, all of them aimed at Syria.

Let's take another look at 1956. There's a striking coincidence here: at the moment Nasser has for many months been showing signs of moderation — very relative, but moderation just the same — with respect to Israel. Nasser talked at Bandung about 'support of the rights of the Arab people of Palestine ... the implementation of the United Nations Resolutions on Palestine [that is, for two states in Palestine, including a Jewish state] and the achievement of a peaceful settlement of the Palestine question.' (This is the text that he submitted and got the conference to adopt.) On 26 August 1956 the head of Nasser's personal cabinet declared, 'As long as there is no *shooting war* Egypt will authorize the passage of Israeli shipping through the Suez Canal, provided that the boats are not transporting military supplies.' Furthermore, since 1955 the fedayeen infiltrations have been coming not from Egypt but from Jordan. Result: Israel launches an offensive against Egypt, with the agreement, backing and complicity of you-know-who.

This is the strange coincidence: Israel goes after the countries that the Western camp primarily targets, independently or almost independently of Israel's own motives. In 1956 it was Egypt. In 1967, *mutatis mutandis*, Syria.

b) Nasser took the initiative of sending the UN forces back and closing the Gulf of Aqaba. Why? Two hypotheses can be put forward. One is that he believed in the threat of an Israeli attack on Syria. The second — the one that I would choose, though the first is not absurd — is that he judged that this was a propitious moment for increasing his prestige, which amounts to saying (given his 'positive role' in the Middle East, which you acknowledge) for weakening the Hashemite and Saudi camp, particularly around the Yemen issue and even the issue of Aden. Now, what will his initiative accomplish (if it succeeds)? It will eliminate the profit that Israel had reaped from its 1956 aggression. The point is that Israel only consented to withdraw its troops after the Sinai campaign on the condition that UN troops replace them. If Nasser were to wipe out the defeat that imperialism inflicted on him in 1956, then I wouldn't see anything in that that could shock us.

c) But they say that closing the Gulf means choking Israel. In terms of Israel's general trade, 5% goes through the port of Eilat. Of course there's oil. But to the best of my knowledge Israel did not live before 1956 like an invalid in the process of being choked. It doesn't seem unthinkable to me for Israel to be supplied once more through Haifa. The closure of the Gulf of Aqaba would be a major blow to Israel, but in no way a fatal one. So let's not talk about any <u>vital</u> Israeli interest in stopping the Egyptians from wresting from them the fruits of their 1956 aggression.

d) Israel is threatening Jordan, Egypt and Syria with spectacular reprisals for the attacks and sabotage carried out by the fedayeen and other Palestinians (note the total destruction of the village of Samoah in November 1966,[7] including the death of 100 or 200 of its inhabitants). But it has in no way been proven that the Syrians, Egyptians etc. control these irregulars. (The reports in the newspaper *Le Monde* seem entirely conclusive on this point.) Naturally it's easy to argue that the Arab propaganda and agitational campaign against Israel sustains or has created the Palestinian refugees' hatred of Israel. I'm willing to consider that. But the reasoning is so familiar: strikes are fomented by agitators, and revolutions by ringleaders. No one ever considers the possibility that frustration feeds on injustice. Suppose that Israel succeeded tomorrow in obtaining the withdrawal of all Palestinian, Egyptian, Syrian, etc. troops from its borders and

---

7   On 13 November 1966 the Israeli armed forces launched a reprisal raid against the village of Samoah (As-Samu) in the West Bank (then under Jordanian jurisdiction) near Hebron. The attack resulted in 18 deaths, over 130 wounded, and more than 125 destroyed houses according to the report submitted to the UN Security Council, which condemned the aggression on 25 November.

the opening of the Gulf of Aqaba. That would not stop the million refugees from hating Israel just as much. Nor would it make the refugees decide to express their feelings only through petitions to the UN (Israel has violated a series of fundamental UN decisions about borders, refugees, etc. all along) or prayers to Allah. The problem would be as great as ever.

3) So this takes us beyond current events and brings us to the heart of the problem: Israeli-Arab relations as they have existed since 1948 and even well before 1948. You posit that Israel 'is in no way a threat to national or socialist revolutions in the Arab countries'. You add, 'I have no problem admitting that Israel is a pawn of American imperialism, though the phrase is exaggerated.' Agreed, the phrase 'pawn of American imperialism' is rude and unnuanced. <u>But it is not false.</u> Then you continue, 'But I wholly fail to see how Israel is holding back Nasser's revolution in Egypt or anywhere else.' Here you contradict yourself: if Israel is, on the whole, an American pawn, then it does and will do everything in its power to prevent revolutions. And this is what it is doing. Let me explain.

Up until now there has not been a socialist revolution in the Arab world. But there have been a few national revolutions. There are also several essentially reactionary and counter-revolutionary states. Let us examine more closely Israel's attitude towards the revolutionary countries (which are not socialist, that goes without saying) and the counter-revolutionary countries.

- Nasserite Egypt: the 1956 aggression was an avowed attempt to bring down a national revolution in collaboration with French and English imperialism.

- Post-Hashemite Iraq as it emerged from the 1958 revolution: Israel has not been able to intervene directly. But at the time when the monarchy was overthrown, Israel called for American intervention in order to bring down the revolutionary regime. Reading the press of that time would prove it. See in any case *Le Monde* of 14 July 1958.

- Syria: a somewhat different case. But no one can deny that
this country is currently moving in a direction that the US finds
disturbing. The presence of Communists in the government is
— unfortunately — no guarantee for socialism. But nonetheless
Syria is far enough 'to the left' to have provoked an 'anti-
Communist' putsch in 1966, which fortunately failed. Today
Syria is Israel's preferred target (see General Rabin's statement
that the 'revolutionaries in Damascus' threaten a̲l̲l̲ Middle
Eastern governments).

- Algeria: the case is all too familiar. Israel could not stop the
country from winning its independence. But the Algerian
revolution was viewed in Israel with nothing but hostility. To
this we must add, besides Israel's support for France at the
UN and the veneration given in Israel to men like Mollet,
the fact that there was military cooperation between French
paratroopers and Israeli paratroopers who went to Algeria for
training. If Israel was not able to do more it really wasn't its
fault.

- We could even cite some supplementary examples. The
support given to Kasavubu, Adoula and Tshombe's troops
against Lumumbaism and the Congolese rebellion by the
inevitable Israeli paratroopers who officially trained and
coached the anti-rebellion paratroopers in concert with the
white mercenaries who were in Leopoldville at the time.[8] Still
another: the financial support that Tom M'boya[9] received from

---

8   Joseph Kasavubu, first president of the independent Congo (Kinshasa,
     formerly Leopoldville), faced the secession of the province of Katanga led
     by Moise Tshombe in 1960-63 and dismissed leftist Prime Minister Patrice
     Lumumba shortly afterwards. Cyrille Adoula and Colonel Joseph Mobutu
     were leaders of the anti-Lumumba forces. Adoula was prime minister from
     1961-64 and Tshombe from 1964, until Mobutu took power as dictator in
     a CIA-backed coup in 1965.
9   M'boya was a Kenyan trade unionist, independence activist and later
     minister under President Jomo Kenyatta. In alliance with Kenyatta, he
     defended pro-Western, pro-market policies against Vice-President Oginga
     Odinga's 'African socialism'. Odinga was later dismissed.

both the American trade unions and Histadrut.[10] And finally, when two Israeli journalists talked about the complicity of the Israeli secret services in kidnapping Ben Barka,[11] they were tried in secret — not exactly a convincing refutation.

OK, let's forget Ben Barka, Tom M'boya, Kasavubu and Mobutu. Israel's attitude towards the Algerian, Egyptian and Iraqi national revolutions and towards Syria proves its fundamentally counter-revolutionary role. Our only crumb of comfort is that Israel has only limited resources at its disposal. But it had enough for its very useful intervention in Egypt. And then Israel's moral support — as an island of democracy and refuge of the persecuted — can also be useful.

After looking at the 'revolutionary' states, we can make the opposite demonstration. Israel cannot intervene to save the shah of Iran or the king of Saudi Arabia. The only puppet, counterrevolutionary state that's within its reach is Hussein's Jordan. Now Israel, which is opposed to any change in the Middle East, considering (rightly or wrongly) that change could only disrupt the existing equilibrium, shows this typically progressive love of the status quo in one case only: Jordan. On several occasions Israeli leaders have declared — and the declarations have been numerous enough that we can speak of a doctrine — that if anyone tried to shake Hussein's throne, and still more if the dear little man was overthrown, Israel would not hesitate to intervene militarily. Where more or less progressive regimes like Nasser's exist, fear of change does not paralyze Israel, which has done its best to get rid of it. The same holds true for Iraq in 1958. In any case, Israel has taken on the role of Jordan's protector.

This is Israel's nefarious role from a socialist standpoint and from the standpoint of the struggle against imperialism. Having said this, I agree with you that Israel is not the Arab peoples'

---

10   The main Israeli trade union federation.
11   A Moroccan radical opposition leader kidnapped in France and killed in 1965.

public enemy number 1. These peoples have their own system of exploitation and international capitalism, within which Israel's role is negligible, to thank for their misery. In this respect I am not in any way following the Arab propaganda that describes Israel as the scapegoat, the main culprit, and so on and so forth. Israel is not the main culprit. But Israel helps imperialism every chance it gets. The fake socialists deny this and punch the air, as they say in English, going on about the kibbutzim (whose role in the Israeli economy and ideology is very limited and in steady decline). You on the other hand don't deny it. You speak of 'condemning the Israelis for their foreign policy, Suez, etc.'. (But that 'etc.' is really very telling.) Yet what conclusion do you draw from this? You state (allow me to be schematic, or rather, if you please, accept my schema, which I think is impregnable, just for a moment): Israel has an imperialist foreign policy (or a policy of supporting imperialism). And from this you conclude that we must nonetheless recognize its right to exist. I'll come back later to this 'right to exist'. But you certainly have to accept that the first proposition, 'Israel has a policy of consistent support for imperialism' (I've cited 4, 5, 6 or 7 examples showing this, and I defy anyone to give any examples suggesting the opposite) should lead to a different conclusion than the affirmation of Israel's right to exist. I don't claim that it should lead to the conclusion that the Arabs have the right to exterminate it. But I repeat, it should lead to some other conclusion. Could you or could you and Marion suggest what this conclusion might be …?

It all makes me think of the arguments that left-wing Zionists or Israelis or Jews regularly make. When you talk to them about Israel's involvement with imperialism, some of them just deny it all outright. Others, more sincere and completely pathetic, say: it's true, we don't like it, but what do you want us to do about it? We have no choice. Do they realize that there could be no more terrible condemnation of Israel than this admission that Israel's alliance with the imperialist camp is inevitable, that

Israel is unfortunately <u>stuck with it</u>? So I ask you one more time, what conclusion should we draw from this alliance? The word alliance is inappropriate by the way. Israel's relationship with imperialism is not an entity's relationship to a category that is external to it. There is not an 'alliance' between Israel and the imperialist camp, the way there was an alliance between the USSR and Nazi Germany. Israel is <u>in</u> the imperialist camp.

We could draw out the discussion by raising the problem of the Israeli situation and the colonial situation. I believe we would come to the following conclusion: there are major differences between the Israeli condition and the condition of South Africa's white minority, or in the past Algeria's. But there are also striking analogies. The only thing is I don't think that this problem is essential to my argument. It would only be useful in analyzing the origins of Israeli imperialism, and showing why it was not the result of accident or just bad luck. At the time when there were real discussions in the socialist movement — I mean before 1914 — there were many controversies on this issue. All Marxists, and I repeat all, agreed at the time that Zionism and the project of Jewish settlement in Palestine, essentially an imperialist and colonial enterprise, could only lead to a confrontation between progressive Arabs and Jewish settlers. But OK, I admit that this is all an old story…

To move on to Israeli rights and particularly Israeli's right to preserve their state, your reasoning is as follows: Israel is doing one bad thing after another, but that does not condemn it to destruction, any more than Vietnam and other filthy doings condemn the US to destruction. The argument seems a bit hasty to me.

I could mention first of all to a Marxist — I mean a Marxist theoretician like you — that Marxism has never analysed the Jewish national phenomenon, of which Israel is an outgrowth, the same way as other national realities. But let's skip that bit once more. The key point is that the analogy between Israel and the US (or *for that matter* Germany) neglects a point that is not a mere detail. Nobody challenges the existence of the American state (the Indians might have, but they haven't been given a chance to challenge anything at all). But it so happens that Arab countries and Arab parties (on the right but also on the left) and Arab peoples (exploited or less exploited, uncultivated but not always all that uncultivated) do challenge the existence of the state of Israel. This is a fact. And shouldn't we ask ourselves how it is that Arab socialists have ended up supporting this position?

What needs to be understood here is that Israel (and the Palestinian Jews before it, but Israel above all) constitutes for the Arabs the very symbol of their humiliation, and furthermore an auxiliary of imperialism and therefore a danger (not Public Enemy No. 1 or even No. 2, but a permanent danger inasmuch as it is an auxiliary of imperialism: witness Suez, Iraq, Syria, etc.). Humiliation and danger, this is what Israel means for Arabs in general. In addition to that, it means wholesale robbery for the million Palestinian refugees to whom Israel definitively, categorically and unconditionally denies the right to go back to their homes — wretched homes now that they have been blown up, razed or occupied by an elite population: Jews who didn't escape from Hitler's camps but rather either from Communist tyranny (particularly Poland and Romania) or from a humiliating coexistence with Arab peoples in whose midst they had until then lived in relative harmony. By removing them [the Jews from Arab countries] from their native lands, where their situation was essentially different from and thus better than European Jews', Israel was not rescuing them from massacres and persecution but rather gathering them in the name of nationalism pure and simple.

To resume: Israel means for the Arabs humiliation, threats and (in some cases) wholesale usurpation. Let me spend a few moments on the humiliation. The Arabs did not want any massive Jewish settlement in Palestine. The Jewish settlers constituted a foreign element there: I mean an element without contacts with the indigenous population, that was ignored or paid insufficient attention to or whose existence was denied. The only relationships were those of the purchaser of the land with the seller of the land (but the seller was the effendi,[12] with the result that in many cases Arab agricultural workers or peasants who had been farming the land that was sold were expelled from it), or in other, more exceptional cases (because Jews were supposed to work with other Jews and prefer Jewish labour — this was the official theory of the Jewish trade unions in the 1920s and '30s) those of bosses to employees. The argument that the Arabs were better off in Palestine under the Mandate (thanks to the Jews) than non-Palestinian Arabs were elsewhere does not hold water of course. How many times have we been told — and it was true to some extent — that the Muslims in Algeria were doing better in French Algeria than the Muslims who didn't have the privilege of living under a French colonial regime...? Anyway, this is one reason why the Palestinians preferred not to have the Jews in their country. There were other reasons, some of them legitimate (on the political level the Jews opposed all the democratic demands made by enlightened, petty bourgeois, Palestinian nationalist sectors; the Jews opposed popular representation in the legislative or executive organs of the Mandate, for example, for fear that the Arab majority would acquire prerogatives that the Jewish minority would suffer from) and others much less legitimate, reeking of the xenophobia that the Palestinians have never had a monopoly of.

The Palestinians would rather not have had these superior, usurping Europeans in their midst. But these Europeans were imposed on them. After the war there was an additional argument: the survivors of the camps had to be saved (on this argument — Israel, country of survivors of the camps — I've done a statistical calculation showing that roughly 10% of the Israeli population comes either from Nazi Germany, from Nazi-occupied countries, or from camps — that's a lot, but just the same it does make the situation clear). But why in God's name, if

---

12   The big landowner.

the fate of the Jews was weighing so on Europeans' consciences, didn't they take on the task of succouring and hosting the survivors themselves? Did all those Jewish survivors want to go to Palestine, by the way? No matter — to Palestine they were sent! The Palestinians themselves, who bear no responsibility for the tragedy, were not consulted. So in 1947 the UN created the Jewish state. The Arabs did not accept this decision. Nor do I think that socialists can confuse this decision with any more or less moral principle of legitimacy. At that time, even more than now, the UN was a European, capitalist, etc. *machin*.[13]

Since that time the Arabs still have not recognized Israel. Why are they so obstinate? After all, all the good souls and realistic minds in the world have been telling them: recognize Israel, because it's a fact. The realists forget that there is another fact too: that the Arabs, the main people whose interests are at stake, do not recognize Israel.

Israel by contrast keeps saying and repeating that it wants peace. This is true. But clearly this peace, meaning Arab recognition of a state that they never wanted to recognize, this peace-as-recognition, would be a huge victory for Israel. The victory. So of course they want peace. If they had the strength to impose this peace (and recognition of their state) on people who want nothing to do with it, then fine, they could go ahead. But the relationship of forces does not permit it. So let them pay a price for this victory; let them say what they are willing to pay for it. But on this point they are strangely silent. Are they willing to return to the 1947 partition boundaries? No. To take back the refugees? Not a chance. Their only offer is to compensate the refugees, if the UN or US lends them the money to do it with. That's just not serious.

Now let's talk about the Arabs. They are sticking to their refusal to recognize the state of Israel, and thus to their 'ill

---

13   The 'gadget' (*machin*) is the contemptuous word used by French General de Gaulle to refer to the UN.

will' of 1947 and before. Note that the whole Israeli policy has never encouraged them to take up a better attitude. Quite the contrary. All the more so because the humiliation persists: the whole image of Israel in the rest of the world is the image of a modern, civilized, technologically advanced, efficient and cultivated nation, and I spare you all the rest of it. But in the context in which it's bestowed, all this praise of Israel (deserved or undeserved) is an implicit, constant criticism of the surrounding environment, because the praise is given with reference to the context. Israel is the example that the Arab world ought to follow — if the Arabs were capable of it; but alas, everything suggests that the example is too noble and exalted and the master too sublime for such backward pupils. This point of view, which it must be said is not a left-wing point of view (though of course it is the standpoint of many, thoroughly European social democrats), forms the very substance of the image that ordinary people have of the respective situations of Israel and its neighbours. Israel is a European beachhead and a bastion of civilization surrounded by a sterile landscape and a dark continent. I believe the Arabs are aware of this contrasted, lunatic imagery that Israel helps to maintain.

31 May

God — I mean Allah — works in all sorts of ways. In this morning's *Le Monde* I see a letter to the editor that illustrates perfectly these two images of civilized Israel and Arab savages. I enclose this foul bit of literature, which is a caricature (though not all that much of one) and still entirely characteristic. This too is Arab humiliation and the role that Israel plays in it.

This concludes this point for me, and I ask myself how anyone could deny that, when all is said and done, Israel appears for the Arab world — and chiefly for the progressive Arab world — as a threat (witness the whole of its foreign policy), a source of humiliation and a cause of wholesale robbery (of the refugees).

This leaves me with one last point to deal with, though admittedly the trickiest one, the only one that people like you can use against the Arabs in this affair, and the only one that undermines the Arabs' case: the challenge to Israel's existence.

The only thing is, after all, your position is a little too facile. Here is a country that, at least if you accept my analysis — but I expect you to challenge it with facts and not with legends and myths about Israel as the land of socialism […] with its collectivist settlements (kibbutzim) and cooperative villages (moshavim) — here is this country Israel that plays a thoroughly nefarious role in all the ways I've listed; here is a country that, all told and whatever you say about it, plays no positive role in the Middle East. The wrongs that it is committing only hurt the Arabs. Given that this country does not seem inclined to make any serious concession, and secondly given that the relationship of forces is being transformed or developing in favour of the Third World that the Arabs are part of and disadvantageously for the Israeli-Western bloc; given that schematically this is the way things look, what right do we have to demand that the Arabs recognize the <u>Israeli political reality</u>? Nasser intimated several times (above all before 1956) that return of the refugees and a return to the 1947 frontiers would open the way to a possible solution. He was never taken at his word. In fact the Arabs are being asked to surrender. It's true that Israel's survival does not prevent the economic, human, socialist development of the Arab world. It doesn't prevent it. It only fetters it; it makes it more difficult (because as you say, Israel, with a nuance more or less, is a 'pawn of American imperialism'). What has to be done to stop this nefarious factor from continuing to play the role of fetter on progress and auxiliary of imperialism? We can hope for change in Israel. But let's not forget after all that the forces of the Israeli left, even if we include the Communists and the Mapam people (great leftists these Mapam people, who not only supported

Suez but had representatives in the government at the time of Suez), represent barely 10% of the population — a 10% that incidentally includes the Arab minority, which generally votes Communist.

I admit that the rest of us — the anti-Israeli left that includes, besides the Communists (for their own particular reasons, no doubt sullied more often than not by opportunism), the Trotskyists and a few serious Marxists — I admit that we don't have any serious answer that can fully satisfy us. The Arabs say: the state of Israel must be destroyed. That's not a good formulation, because it opens the door to all sorts of hypotheses — including, wrongly I think, the hypothesis of exterminating 2 million Israelis. The only thing is, this is a rather gratuitous interpretation. No official, serious declaration corroborates it. But no official, serious declaration rules it out either. Therefore the Arabs have the responsibility of saying what they mean and what they want. But there are other hypotheses besides extermination (which is the most improbable hypothesis; it is explicitly rejected by some Arabs, and I'm not familiar enough with the whole set of Nasserite declarations to say whether Nasser himself didn't explicitly exclude it at some point). They need to clarify what they mean by destroying a state.

- Do they mean physical destruction; does 'state' here mean 'nation'?
- Do they mean destroying the Israeli political entity as it exists today and replacing it with a different set-up: for example, transforming it into a federative component of a Middle Eastern federation, in which the Israeli nation would take part?
- Do they mean creating a Palestinian state in which Jews would be nothing more than citizens with individual rights, without national representation? (But in that case there would be 2 million Jews and 1 million Arabs in this state, after the necessary and legitimate return of the refugees.)
- Do they mean creating a Palestinian state from which the Jews would be expelled?

All these hypotheses are plausible, some more than others. It
is time for the Arabs — I mean the responsible leaders and
in particular the organizations and men of the left (Egyptian
Marxists or socialists, some of the Ba'athist tendencies,[14] the
Moroccan UNFP,[15] elements of the Algerian FLN, which — is it
a regrettable mistake on their part, or a mere coincidence? — are
all anti-Israeli) to explain themselves clearly. They are not doing
it (at least as far as I know, but it would be worth doing a survey
to see if statements haven't been made to some sparse extent),
I'm afraid because they themselves don't know how the problem
can be resolved. They share our own uncertainty.

Our uncertainty, I say. Of course, I think the best solution
would be incorporating the Israeli nation — since it exists
as a cultural and geographical entity (very different by the
way from the Jewish entity) — into a federal whole. But this
strikes me as extraordinarily difficult to achieve. It's almost
utopian. But perhaps not entirely. All we can hope is that
small steps can gradually be taken that bring us closer. What I
would like to see on the Arab side — that is, from the left-wing
minority or socialists — would be an essential contribution
(clearly outlining a solution that rules out extermination,
which though they are anti-Israeli they can neither desire nor
envisage) moving in this direction. And something else would
be necessary just the same as well from the Israeli side and the
leftists who support Israel. Until now Mapam (to take the best
Israeli example except for the Communists) have proposed
nothing and rejected the refugees' return. The *New Outlook*
people [linked to Mapam] are particularly empty-headed and
in fact hypocritical. They're for peace. All Israelis are for peace.
They're for Israeli-Arab brotherhood, and this sets them apart

---

14   During the sixties, some circles within the Arab nationalist tradition —
     including elements within the Ba'ath party — moved toward Marxism,
     most of them to the point of breaking with their original movement.
15   UNFP: National Union of Popular Forces, a Moroccan left-wing nationalist
     party.

from their compatriots. But as long as they don't make any real concessions, all that is just sentimental verbiage.

My ad hominem conclusion: the position that the two of you have is neither solid, nor well founded (I'm not saying that my position is flawless), nor even — I'm sorry to say it — serious. In everything you say you confirm a series of findings of fact: despite reservations, the pro-imperialist character of Israel; despite reservations, the positive character of Nasserism. But you don't draw any conclusion from them. And the only imperative that you affirm, it seems to me, is Israel's survival, without your seeing the need to clarify what you mean by that. If only you put forward two postulates and two imperatives: 1) the necessity of anti-imperialist struggle, and 2) the survival of Israel (while clarifying what you mean by that). If only in addition you would try to clarify the relationship between these two points. But no. What emerges from your letter [Ralph] is a position you share with a whole moderately pro-Israeli, but in the end definitely pro-Israeli, left: there is only one imperative for you: Israel's survival. Without any details.

When one day the problem is raised of the survival of the South African state (and I'm not claiming that the Israelis' role in the Arab world can be identified with the South African whites' relationship to 'their' blacks — far from it), it will be our duty to reject the solution of exterminating those white bastards. But having said this, have we solved the problem...? If this is all we say, we're just sentimentalists and nothing more (even if the sentiment is justified). You two, in limiting yourself to saying, in this episode of the Israeli-Arab conflict as in all the previous episodes and all the episodes still to come: Israel must survive — the rest consisting only of reservations, not about the nature of the Israeli state, but rather about its policies, reservations from which you seem to draw no consequences whatsoever — by sticking to this position, you are being sentimentalists and nothing more. While the Israeli question includes for us a series of factors, and among them is one factor called Auschwitz, let's

grant the Arabs just the same the right to give a very low priority
to this factor, which is so foreign to their own direct or indirect
experience.

On the question of Israel, to sum it all up — and, it goes
without saying, without wanting to put your intentions on
trial (not your intentions [Ralph]; but it's a different matter for
the thousands of pro-Israelis who surround us) — I'm afraid
that you are reacting as a European and a Jew rather than as a
socialist. If the discussion were about any other nation playing
the role that Israel is playing, you would have different standards
than the ones you have for 'our brothers'. At least, I think so.
But when it comes to Israel, you, an intellectually and politically
intransigent man of the left, who is concerned not only with
declaring principles but also with bringing about victory in a
concrete struggle — about Israel, you write: let us condemn
the Israelis' foreign policy. This formal condemnation doesn't
amount to much, comrade. There are two things missing
from it: first, you should try to make a connection between
Israel's foreign policy and the nature of this state. (After all it's
no accident that Israel's <u>whole</u> foreign policy is noxious. We
can judge it to be more or less noxious; we can be harsher or
less harsh in our judgment on this policy; but it is definitely,
essentially, existentially <u>noxious</u>. The facts are there. We can
explain this noxious policy and make excuses for it. But I defy
anyone to find me any positive facts, <u>one</u> positive attitude, in any
area at all of Israeli foreign policy.) And then you must clarify
what it means for you to 'condemn' Israel's foreign policy. When
you condemn US policies (and I see quite well that these two
cases, Israel and the US, are qualitatively different), you propose
expressing this condemnation in a certain kind of struggle.
When you condemn Wilson's policies, Labourism, Gaullism
or God knows what, you look for ways to do something
about them and means of fighting them. That's a political
condemnation. But in Israel's case, I do see a condemnation
(of its 'foreign policy', expressed parenthetically you might say

without reference to the nature of the Israeli enterprise), but I
don't see what concrete meaning it has for you.

A few more final remarks — apologizing and asking your
forbearance for the disproportionate length of it all, but it
weighs on my heart.

a) Your 'pro-Israelism' leads you, dear Ralph, where it is
leading quite a few people these days: to an 'anti-communist'
position. (The inverted commas are for you; for other people
they're superfluous.) 'I think it's quite amusing', you write, 'that
the world Communist left — the Chinese, the Russians, etc.
— should have finally managed to agree on ... backing Nasser
to the bitter end. This support falls into the category of the most
total opportunism, and is the same kind of reflex that made
them support Sukarno and his national revolution.'

I disagree with you completely on this point. When we judge
the Communists' support of Nasser, in my opinion we have
to look at what they're supporting him against. And you
make a comparison with Sukarno. I admit that I'm not very
up-to-date on the problems of the Malaysian federation with
Singapore. But unless I'm mistaken, the Communists were
right to support Indonesia in its conflict with Malaysia. They
were of course wrong to support Sukarno as the leader of the
Indonesian nationalist bourgeoisie. Now what is at stake in
the Arab-Israeli conflict? Is Nasser's current struggle directed
against the proletariat, against his own proletariat, or against a
proletarian nation? Can this current business be summed up
as a choice between Nasser (the national bourgeoisie) and class
struggle? Obviously not. So the comparison with Sukarno has
no relevance.

Clearly Communist opportunism exists and is absolutely
repugnant. (Unless I'm wrong, that eminent hangman the shah
of Iran is taking his ease in the USSR right now.) But in this case
Communist opportunism was on display when the USSR voted
in favour of the creation of the state of Israel, thus breaking

with its constant attitude and with what Marxism, incidentally, had always said about the Zionist phenomenon. When there is a fight between Nasser and the left, a clash between Nasser and the Communists whom he throws into jail, then of course we have to be against Nasser. But the fight waged by <u>some</u> Arab countries against Israel is a fight (which can be fought well or badly, by appropriate or inappropriate means — that we can discuss, and I'm far from sure that their means are appropriate) not against the left but rather against <u>the right</u>.

And since you're talking about the international Communist camp, which has lined up as a bloc behind the Arabs, do you really, honestly believe that this is only opportunism? I refuse to believe it. Chinese opportunism (which exists) is after all not as far advanced as Soviet opportunism. When we speak, as you do, about Israel's foreign policy, how can anyone be surprised or indignant or attribute the socialist camp's hostility to this state to pure opportunism? Really, I don't understand.

b) One last time I will examine one of your sentences, and we could stop there: 'It is no duty of socialists to support pseudo-socialist revolutions <u>unconditionally</u> [your emphasis]; they should do it in a nuanced way.'

Very well. It may be that my support for Nasser and the camp of <u>some</u> Arabs (I have no more use for Hussein, Feisal, the shah, etc. than you do), while certainly not unconditional, is not couched with enough reservations or nuances. That's possible. But my position is one of non-unconditional support for the Arabs in the Israeli case. Nothing in your letter suggests, despite the statement that I've just quoted, that you have the same position (once again, even with nuances). You take your stand on the side of Israel (except for a few nuances), putting forward one <u>single</u> imperative: Israel's survival. This is one of the contradictions that I see in your position.

c) One very last thing: I support unconditionally the Vietnamese struggle and, when it occurs, the Latin American struggle

against American imperialism. This struggle nonetheless
probably increases the danger of a world war. But on this point
there is nothing to be done. If the Arabs, in their just struggle
against Israel, create the danger of a global conflagration (just
as Israel does with its unjust attitude towards the Arab world),
then they're wrong, and are playing an irresponsible 'game'.
But once more, in the name of our wisdom, in the name of our
detachment and from the height of our pedantry, what way can
we suggest for them to fight against Israel, which to them means
humiliation, threats and usurpation…?
I'm done. I know at least one thing: that is that in August 1914
I would not have succumbed to patriotism. And yet God knows
that I feel Jewish in all sorts of ways.…

Latest news on another front: I've passed some medical tests. I
haven't yet recovered, although things are going better. These
last few days I had taken a few liberties with the doctors' orders,
for example working seated at my desk (what a delight). To
which this interminable letter bears witness. Doctor's orders:
back to bed for at least two weeks. […]
I hope to read a letter from you again soon.

Affectionate regards to you both,

Marcel

[*Letterhead: London School of Economics and Political Science*]

2 June 1967

Dear Marcel

The most economical way to respond to your letter, if not the most elegant, is to comment *as I go along*, and take stock of the argument along the way:

1. Arab socialism: let's not rush past this too quickly, despite our apparent agreement. It's good to remind ourselves that these are essentially nationalist movements with very meagre, even non-existent ideological content, that employ socialist rhetoric the same way that all the African regimes do. This is not merely a question of pedantry and nomenclature. On the contrary, this situates the goals and very nature of the confrontation with Israel in a very important way. By this I mean that there is a very clear intention at work of exacerbating nationalist feeling in a chauvinist and narrow-minded form, rather than making it a vehicle for socialism; and of using Israel to this end. The only thing that really makes me doubt the Arab will to liquidate Israel is that if Israel didn't exist they would have to invent it. Nationalist feeling, even of this kind, has a positive, anti-imperialist side to it (as I said before, or rather in my last letter), but the fact remains that a case must still be made that Israel poses any threat to the national/anti-imperialist thrust of these dictatorial, bureaucratic, military, demagogically populist — in short, very ambiguous — regimes (people have been arguing about the real nature of Nasserism for years). I'll come back to this.

2. By contrast to your qualified approval of Arab 'socialism', you

have no use for Israel, this 'peaceful, progressive, democratic, quasi-socialist islet' — in certain respects quite rightly. But one mustn't exaggerate. After all, it is the only country in the Middle East where a certain freedom of expression exists, along with other 'bourgeois freedoms' that we value so cheaply — including, a paradox that you will appreciate, the fact that it is the only country in the region with a legal Communist party, in fact two. Arabs are discriminated against there — no doubt. But how many Israelis protest against this, and without getting thrown in jail? After all, persecutions of Jews in the Arab world have not, to the best of my knowledge, elicited many Arab protests of the same kind. This leads to a simple factual observation — since you're the one carrying on about the myth of democratic Israel and so forth — that there are certain aspects of Israeli life and politics that do not compare all that unfavourably with their counterparts in the Arab world, everywhere in the Arab world. I don't understand your determination to heap abuse on every aspect of Israeli politics in such a passionate way. Personally I believe I see things with a bit more detachment. But I'll come back to this point as well.

3. General Rabin's remarks about Syria are in truth sinister, and I disapprove of them; they seem more lunatic than sinister, at least if no decision has been made in fact to march on Damascus. Even the hundreds of Syrian raids on Israel wouldn't justify an outright invasion. But what must a state do that is systematically attacked the way that Syria has attacked Israel in recent months? Just accept it unflinchingly? Carry out reprisals? It's hard to say, I agree. But it's not a problem that can be evaded. And there is no doubt about the continual Syrian provocations, I believe?

4. Your explanation of Nasser's motives in closing off the Gulf of Aqaba leaves something to be desired: you put forward the hypothesis that his goal is 'weakening the Hashemite and Saudi camp'. No doubt you wrote this before the Jordanian 'royal brother''s visit to Cairo. Doesn't this manifest error on your part make you think about the nature of the Nasserite challenge and

the limits of Nasserite progressivism, which is willing to align itself with all the Arab regimes in an Arab 'holy war'? I repeat, there are positive sides to this Arab <u>nationalism,</u> as there were to African nationalism in the 1950s when it was directed against Westerners. But 'socialism' has very little to do with it, and in some cases nothing.

You think it's very remarkable that Israel chooses Syria first of all to get angry at. There's nothing remarkable about it. They hoped that the Jordanians would be a less dangerous element because of their hatred of Nasserism. A miscalculation. But not a very remarkable one.

5. Admittedly, Nasser has taken back the fruits of Israeli aggression. But much as I condemn the aggression, it seems to me that this taking back can only mean an attempt at strangulation in a war without quarter. You say the 'closure of the Gulf of Aqaba would be a major blow to Israel, but in no way a fatal one'. I suppose you're right. But <u>why</u> stop Israel from using this port, if not out of determination to weaken it? What <u>danger</u> does Eilat represent for the Arab world? None in fact.

6. Are you seriously suggesting that the incessant raids on Israel are taking place without the consent of the governments involved? The idea strikes me as completely absurd. Poor Egyptian, Syrian etc. governments, that can't stop these things from happening. Asinine, my dear friend. Have these governments ever disavowed the raids — one single raid? Here you are falling into the worst kind of bias.

7. What you say about Israel's foreign policy seems right to me, and I say it myself. But what strikes me very much is the way you transform an <u>attitude</u> into a <u>role</u>. Of course there are examples, like the ones you give, of Israeli intervention into Arab affairs. But all this is of minor importance in the perspective of the general Arab liberation movement; it amounts to very little. If Israel had the means it might amount to more; but it doesn't. If Israel were a country of 25,000,000 people, it would be a

real bastion of Western imperialism in the Middle East. But in that case no one would be talking about liquidating it. None of this is the case. Therefore all those Israeli 'declarations' are laughably insignificant. They're stupid of the Israelis, worthy of condemnation, as is any support for imperialism; but to treat them as a key or even serious element in the Western struggle against Arab liberation, whatever the limits of that liberation, looks like self-delusion in your case and pure and simple mystification in the case of the Arab leaders.

Then there is the not insignificant fact, however regrettable it may be, that Israel's foreign policy was imposed on it wholly as a result of the implacable hostility that the Arab world has always manifested towards it. This could be the topic of a long discussion; but your inclination is to neglect <u>anything</u> that might extenuate Israel's faults and crimes or even explain them. *Tout comprendre n'est pas tout pardonner.* But why not admit that there weren't all that many alternatives?

8. You ask me what conclusion should be drawn from Israeli policies. My conclusion is very simple: nothing more than that Israel should change its policies, and that circumstances and the neighbouring countries should make this possible. There's no big problem here. As long as the Arab world directly threatens Israel's existence — and the idea that this is not the case is absurd — this country will remain in the imperialist camp, if that is in fact its place, and I would agree with you, but with certain rather serious qualifications. After all, a change in orientation is not something that a state does on its own without any changes elsewhere. And <u>once the state of Israel was established</u>, over the Arab world's opposition, the idea that they shouldn't have gone looking for alliances etc. is rather abstract. It is in fact Israel's great historic misfortune, which may yet cost it its existence, that no alliances were available to it outside the imperialist camp. Even then, they should have looked for another way out. But we are dealing with people who aren't socialists, or not the right kind.

9. Saying that Israel is in the imperialist camp is one thing; speaking of Israeli imperialism as you do is something else again. This imperialism consists, it seems to me, in wanting to defend its borders against hostile neighbours. There are no doubt Israelis, even in high places, who would like to annex a good chunk of Jordan, which is reprehensible. But are there serious Israeli plans to conquer and subjugate Arab people outside its territory? *Nonsense.* Speaking of Israel as an imperialist state seems to me another piece of evidence of an extraordinary bias. (I've just reread your paragraph about Israel and Jordan, in which you describe Israel as Hussein's 'protector'. You couldn't have known that it would be Nasser who turned out to be Hussein's protector. But I repeat, this kind of judgment suggests that your perspective requires re-examination.)

10. You describe Israel as a 'permanent danger' to the Arab countries, as an auxiliary of imperialism. You even underscore it. *Nonsense.* Is there the least doubt that if Israel hadn't been threatened since it first came into existence, it would not have taken on the role of auxiliary of imperialism; and that even now, the idea that Israel is a threat to Arab liberation is absolutely preposterous? If you really think the Americans need Israel to oppose Arab liberation, you've gone off the rails. It would be a pretty poor auxiliary that doesn't give you any bases, that isn't part of any alliance, etc., and focuses all its policies on what it can't help seeing as a deadly threat, and as a result of that clings to the Americans. This idea of an auxiliary is quite useful. But when you think about it seriously, it carries very little conviction. Except in the case of Suez (against American opposition — some auxiliary!), when the Israelis clung to French and English imperialism, which was a crime and a mistake at the same time.

11. For the Arabs Israel means humiliation etc. This brings us finally to the fundamental problem, that is, the existence of Israel. You yourself say that the Arabs reject it outright. This is true, and the very core of the problem. Then, the next day, you

seem to suggest that for Nasser this isn't the case. This seems
to me rather dubious. But at this point your line of argument,
not very surprisingly, becomes rather verbose. You doubt that
the will to extermination exists. But does or <u>can</u> the liquidation
of Israel, the avowed objective of the Arab countries, mean
anything else, given the Israelis' resolve not to let themselves
be liquidated? When the Arabs' avowed goals cannot be
attained without extermination, saying that there is no will to
extermination strikes me as a poor argument.

You ask what right the Jews have to be in Palestine; or rather,
to found a state in Palestine. The question doesn't seem to me
to lend itself to a satisfactory answer, because it doesn't mean
much. Their right stems from the fact that the world is what it
is, from Hitler's persecutions, etc. etc. All this doesn't amount
to an answer. <u>But the fact is there.</u> And what also needs to
be emphasized, as you say yourself, is that the Israelis are in
your eyes only a 'fetter', they only make the economic, human
and socialist development of the Arab world more difficult.
Personally I don't think that argument is worth much; but the
fact remains that even by your interpretation Israel isn't a real
obstacle to what is to be desired, a flourishing of the region.
Incidentally this should dispose of your South African analogy,
which seems quite pitiful to me: in South Africa 3,000,000
whites physically hinder the blacks' development, oppress them,
etc. The Israelis aren't oppressing 40 million Arabs; at the very
most, as I said earlier, they are discriminating (reprehensibly)
against their own 200,000 (is this the right figure?) Arabs. This is
why it seems possible to me, <u>leaving aside all the rest,</u> to see the
survival of the Israeli state as a valid objective.

There remains the refugee issue. First of all, we may note that
the refugees could have been absorbed into the Arab world over
the past 20 years, just like the Germans expelled by the Poles
from Poland's 'liberated territories'. Who on the left, *incidentally,*
supports the German refugee organizations? No one. All these
analogies are doubtless flawed. But my analogies seem to me

at least as convincing as yours. Nevertheless, it is true just the
same that a solution would have to be found: reintegration,
compensation, etc. And if the Arabs seriously asked for it and
raised it in negotiations, they should be supported; but they
would also have to recognize the state of Israel. This means that
the two things shouldn't be mixed together as you've done. This
means that I posit the existence of an Israeli state with an Israeli
majority. One day I hope, just as in Europe or Latin America,
larger entities than these national states will be built. Until then I
posit the existence of the Israeli state, not out of Zionism etc. (all
that is very much out of date now that the state of Israel exists,
which makes what the great thinkers of the 2nd International
said of little relevance), but simply out of recognition of a reality
whose disappearance would be a terrible catastrophe given
the only current conditions in which it could disappear. All
your hypotheses rule out the existence of Israel; and in fact in
the current circumstances these hypotheses are null and void,
abstract constructions. There are only two alternatives, only two:
either this state survives, or it is liquidated. The modalities of
these two alternatives may vary (for instance the state survives
but reabsorbs a number of refugees; or it is liquidated but not
all the Jews are exterminated, meaning that a great number
of them are only 'expelled' from a new Palestinian state), but
these are still the only two alternatives. All your sermons about
the necessity of the Arabs' studying the issue etc. and making
their proposals unfortunately don't change anything. One
day this will indeed have to be done, or even now if you like.
But this isn't the immediate problem, or even the one that the
Arab leaders want to pose. Therefore a choice must be made
between the two alternatives: either support Israel's continued
existence, with whatever criticisms and qualifications you like;
or, as you do in your hypotheses, envisage Israel's liquidation,
with everything that has to mean for those who wish to oppose
this destruction, meaning most Israelis, including the ones in
Mapam and the Communist parties.

Here no doubt an emotional element enters into play. As a Jew, I would find this eventuality awful; that is, as a Jew, I would see the massacre of an indeterminate number of Jews and the expulsion of the rest as something atrocious, in light of the history of so many Jews in Israel — an event that would have the dimensions, if not the numbers, of Hitler's massacres. I say 'as a Jew' so as not to delude myself. And yet I hope with all my heart and mind that it isn't as a Jew that I would find this awful, but as a socialist, that is, as someone who is bound to seek human measurements in order to judge historical events. After all many non-Jews who are neither Mollet nor Eden nor imperialist stooges share this point of view. All at once you loathe the whole left, that is the whole non-Communist left, 'from Sartre to Guy Mollet' (I find this kind of amalgam, coming from you, stupefying; it makes me think that you're approaching these issues with an extraordinary bias ... 'from Sartre to Guy Mollet' — that's unworthy of you). But the other left, the left of Kosygin[16] & Co. — do you find them appetizing now, these opportunists who have discovered a new Arab vocation for themselves, with the Communist parties of the world? Take note that in my opinion the unctuous statements in *L'Humanité* that a settlement 'should not put in question etc. [Israel's existence]' are pure hypocrisy. How can anyone support the Arab leaders' avowed positions without accepting their desire to liquidate Israel? If this is not the case, if the words attributed by *Le Monde* to the Egyptian 'authorities' are true, I would be thrilled, I assure you, not to speak of Marion. But this seems to me a very forlorn hope. I only hope that the Israelis won't do anything to make things worse, even if this means their losing Eilat. But I'm very afraid that they will make their move and become 'aggressors', meaning that they'll try to take back Eilat, or rather to unblock the Gulf.

---

16   Andrei Kosygin, Soviet prime minister from 1964 to 1980.

I have read the dispatch from Havana.[17] There's nothing
surprising there. There is a big current under way that any
Communist leader feels compelled to swim with, the current
of Arab liberation. I'm pulled in the same direction myself; but
since I'm not a Communist leader I don't have to carry their flag
but can allow myself the luxury of political honesty, that is of
stating nuances. The opportunism is above all the responsibility
of the Russians and the European Communist parties: the
Russians because they want only to get what they can out of
the business, while I think keeping an eye on Vietnam; the
Communist parties who neither can nor want to do anything
but follow the Russians.

Your particular case is of course different. You are caught up in
pro-Arab schematism. This is a long-standing problem, and I
can only remind you of your Algerian illusions, which by the
way you induced me to share, though I don't hold that against
you. And you are also caught up in systematic, passionate,
committed anti-Israelism. I don't understand it. You even go as
far as attacking the Israelis furiously for having a higher cultural
level than the Arabs and thus inducing a feeling of humiliation
in them. It isn't Jewish racism that you seem to condemn
— which should be condemned — but the very fact, which
seems indisputable to me, that the Israeli level of development is
higher than the Arab world's.

I don't claim to be objective while you are subjective. But I
think I'm a good deal more open-minded than you are. Your

17   Marcel Liebman had sent the following dispatch with his letter of 30-31
     May 1967:
     Bulletin from Agence France-Presse: 'Havana, 30 May. "The situation in the
     Middle East is part of the worldwide imperialist escalation that is visible in
     Vietnam, North Korea, Greece and Latin America", writes the newspaper
     Granma, organ of the Cuban CP, in its first commentary on the Israeli-
     Arab conflict. The newspaper declares that Cuba is taking a categorical
     position in favour of Syria and the U.A.R., and assures the Palestinian
     Arab refugees who are fighting to win back their usurped rights of Cuba's
     comradely solidarity. Finally, the newspaper condemns "the way Israel is
     being used as the spearhead of Yankee imperialism".'

bias alarms me, I repeat one more time, simply because it seems to me to skew your perspective and make you see things in a distorted way. You tell me my positions are facile and 'not serious'. I don't know what that means — just that they don't match yours? I on the contrary think they are serious and not at all facile. And I don't have instantaneous solutions — just as nobody else does. But my positions do at least rule out a solution that seems unacceptable to me. Morally and politically, the fact that your positions, far from ruling out this solution, make it inevitable seems lamentable to me, and unacceptable from a socialist point of view. Take note as well that Communists the world over and many Arabs will shed crocodile tears when they witness the Israelis being exterminated and expelled and will say in chorus, 'But this isn't what we wanted — on the contrary, remember, we said that the existence of the state wasn't in question.' That won't be much use. The grass will grow back, no doubt, but I'm not inclined to join this chorus.

All this is very rambling and no doubt full of holes. But the essence of the issue seems clear to me. I add that reading the *Jewish Chronicle* today with its stupid bluster disgusts me as much as it does you. And I would consider an Israeli attack, beyond the shadow of a doubt, a catastrophe. But I still refuse to ignore the reality of the existence of this state or to accept its disappearance.

Between us the discussing isn't meant to *score points*, but to see what the just solution is, that is the socialist solution, taking account of the facts. From this point of view I think my arguments are preferable to yours.

[…]

Your friend

Ralph

[*Letterhead: Clos des Pommiers Fleuris*]

Brussels, 5 June 1967

Dear Ralph,

To reply or not to reply? I'm replying, but maybe I'm wrong.
Perhaps my letter was impassioned. But you award me points:
you're more this than I, I'm more that than you. It doesn't make
much sense. If I'm impassioned, in any event it's not because
I'm an anti-Semite (I hope that that at least is still taken for
granted). As for my attachment to the 'Arab cause', it results
from neither personal friendships nor cultural affinities. Your
passion comes from the fact that you're Jewish, plus some
Israeli connections. But let's stop these arguments (if they're ad
hominem arguments); they lead nowhere. I will however say this
about my 'mistake' in the Algerian business. It's true, I had some
illusions. We've all had illusions, we all have illusions — about
Algeria, about all the Algeria's, the USSR and its development,
the wonderful 1960s and the prospects they would bring for
the anti-imperialist struggle. These illusions are our hopes
as men of the left and our *raison d'être*. I made you share my
illusions about Algeria! *So sorry.* But what I was able to do for
the Algerians, as I told you already, I believe, and repeat because
it's true, was not because I was betting on socialism in Algeria.
It was because here (I mean in Belgium, which geographically
and politically is so close to France), the concrete question was
posed of struggling for an oppressed people, a people oppressed
by another people in a country where the bourgeois democracy
that you urge me not to underestimate was flourishing. For men
of the left in France, but also in Belgium, the Algerian business
was crucial; it enabled us to see how many of us there were

and what good we were. And I'm not about to forget that all those left-wing pro-Israelis (starting with Mapam's official or unofficial representatives) didn't want to do anything to help the Algerians: nothing political, nothing humanitarian. They didn't provide shelter for Algerians; they didn't provide medicines for Algerian refugees. Nothing. And in Israel it was the same story. Yet Algeria was not threatening Israel; the FLN was not anti-Semitic, on the contrary. The French settlers were anti-Semitic. I take responsibility for my illusions about Algeria's future (and this future is still open). My illusions are the illusions of a man of the left. Let the Israelis and pro-Israelis take responsibility for their refusal to do anything at all for the oppressed Algerians struggling against the torturers' colonialism, and for their refusal to openly denounce the Israeli-French alliance. Their refusal was the refusal of frightened nationalists and a hypocritical left. Let everyone take responsibility for his own acts.

But now it's the guns' turn to speak. That's the crushing reality, and it's pushing a solution to the Israeli-Arab problem still further into the future. And there is little doubt that what we're seeing is Israeli aggression. On 2 June you thought it was likely; now it's happening. Israel always said that closing the Gulf of Aqaba would be a *casus belli*, while Nasser said that he would only attack in response to an Israeli attack. Nasser could be content with the gains he had made. But then when on 2 June [Moshe] Dayan and [Menahem] Begin became ministers [in the new Israeli cabinet], it's no surprise that the hard line has won out.

I spent several days not only answering (no doubt in an impassioned way) your letter of a week ago, but also in thinking about the issue. I read everything I could get hold of, and developed some positive ideas for a rather long article that a big-circulation Belgian monthly is going to publish, and for a speech I have to make to the UGS [Union of the Socialist Left] where the two clans are clashing, as they were bound to. The results of my thinking are the following conclusions, which you will no doubt consider utopian, impassioned and dumb, but which I pass on to you just the same.

To get out of this spiral (but the Israeli attack — which was absolutely not authorized under international law, but you'll tell me that these juridical rules aren't a decisive argument for us, and I agree entirely; while the closing of the Gulf was not strangling Israel as it claimed; and above all when Israel had done nothing to explore a peaceful way to solve the conflict — the Israeli attack makes getting out of the spiral more problematic than ever), two symmetrical conditions are necessary:

a) On the Arab side, recognizing the Israeli nation's right to exist. This would open up possibilities for quite a number of solutions, putting in question the current structures of the Israeli state while ruling out solutions of extermination, liquidation, etc.

b) On the Israeli side, recognizing that an injustice has been committed in the Israeli-Arab conflict whose consequences the Arabs, and the Palestinians in particular, are continuing to suffer from, and admitting that this injustice must be made good. Israel has never expressed itself in this way. It denies any injustice, rejects any idea of reparations or even slightly serious concessions. In this case, can't people understand that denying the Arabs anything leads them to demand everything? I have never heard the Israelis, or even any Israelis say: recognize Israel's right to exist (even as a state) and we'll discuss genuine reparations and make concessions. While on the Arab side people at least sometimes envisage making this concession — because of course it would be a concession — of recognizing Israel, the same is not true on the Israeli side.

In fact Nasser has repeatedly envisaged the possibility of recognizing Israel. He did it again just recently. He has often talked about the 1947 frontiers; he has often talked about the return of the refugees and application of all the UN resolutions

(thus including a Palestinian Arab state, internationalization
of Jerusalem, return of those refugees who wish to return but
<u>also</u> creation of a Jewish state). Should he be believed? I don't
say he should. But he should have been taken at his word.
Instead of which the Israelis have always said, we want peace,
but we will never take back the refugees and we will never
accept a modification of the frontiers. But then what will they
accept? If they won't accept anything but being recognized,
what do they expect to happen on the Arab side…? I'll mention
here a personal testimony, for whatever it's worth. I say that
Nasser is relatively moderate. When I met Nahum Goldmann,
[president of the World Jewish Congress and the World Zionist
Organization] and unconditional defender of Israel and all that
(this happened in 1961), he said to me: 'It's impossible for Israel
to reach an understanding with the Algerian revolutionaries
(because he too shared my illusions). The only hope is to
reach an understanding with Nasser.' And he added why he
considered Nasser a moderate, a reasonable man, etc. Obviously
he was speaking in private; in public he expressed himself with
more circumspection. But it's significant just the same. But
Israel's only response was its attack on Egypt and its imbecilic
invective against Nasser/Hitler. Now this will intensify. Who's
responsible…?

1. I won't discuss the merits and ways of 'Arab progressivism'.
I haven't sung its praises. For your part you recognize the
merits of the Nasserite regime. But you describe it as follows:
'dictatorial, bureaucratic, military, demagogically populist'. It's
all of that. But if you grant it a positive character, it must be
something else as well. What then?

2. Your comparison between Israeli bourgeois democracy
where there is freedom of expression (except for the Arabs:
there are 240,000 of them and they don't have a single daily
newspaper or magazine) etc. — a bourgeois democracy 'certain
aspects [of which] do not compare all that unfavourably with
their counterparts in the Arab world' — doesn't stand up to

examination. In 1956 French or British bourgeois democracy didn't compare any more unfavourably with Nasserite Egypt, where there was no CP and were no more democratic freedoms than there are today. Yet this comparison didn't stop you then from being against Britain, France and no doubt Israel as well.

3. Rabin: to your mind his statements aren't so much sinister as lunatic. To my mind they're not lunatic at all. They're only sinister. Would you like another piece of evidence: in December 1966 this same Rabin defined the Israeli attitude towards Syria at the moment of an attempted coup against the Syrian regime, a coup that was a notorious anti-communist power play. He said that 'as for Syria, the essential problem is that of a clash with the regime'. And he went on to compare Israel's role in relation to Syria to the role Israel had adopted to Egypt in 1956. On this same subject you write, 'Are you seriously suggesting that the incessant raids on Israel are taking place without the consent of the governments involved? The idea strikes me as completely absurd…. Asinine, my dear friend.' You are mistaken: I am suggesting nothing and asserting nothing. It's the correspondents of *Le Monde* (which you have to admit is not a pro-Arab newspaper, but rather a pro-Israeli one), all of them, who have not only suggested this but confirmed it. And it's the editors of *Le Monde* in Paris, and perhaps even editor-in-chief Beuve-Méry himself, who have reiterated the statement in their own name. If someone's an ass here, I'm not the one; they are, he is.

4. My explanation of Nasser's motives for closing the Gulf of Aqaba is, you say, a 'manifest error'. I explained nothing. If I remember correctly — impassioned spirit that I am, totally lacking in nuance, siding unconditionally with the Arab camp — I put forward three HYPOTHESES. (1) Nasser's move was a response to a possible or probable Israeli threat to Syria. (2) Nasser was claiming a political victory by challenging the gains Israel had won from Egypt through its 1956 aggression. (3) — as a corollary to (2) — he wanted a diplomatic and political

victory in order to reinforce the prestige and strength of the
Nasserite camp relative to the Hashemite camp. You think the
alliance between Nasser and Hussein proves this hypothesis false.
That's possible. But what makes you assert this so categorically?
First, we don't know to whose advantage this new alliance will
work out. It could increase and 'free up' the strength of Nasserite
forces in Jordan. It's an unlikely hypothesis, I admit, but not
one to be ruled out. But in addition and above all: on day X
Nasser takes one or more measures that end up increasing his
prestige in the Arab world, which weakens the Hashemite camp.
On day X+10 he signs an alliance with Hussein, due to further
development of the situation and new threats that face him.
There's nothing impossible in that. Having said this, whether
or not closing the Gulf of Aqaba wipes out the gains Israel won
through its 1956 aggression, it does in fact among other things
show a 'determination to weaken' Israel, as you say. But it doesn't
strike me as particularly scandalous or even illegitimate for
Egypt, in its conflict with Israel, to try to weaken it.

5. Incidentally, what made you conclude that I 'loathe the
non-Communist left'? That's a peculiar twist. I'm part of the
non-Communist left. I'm talking about the Zionist front from
Sartre to Mollet. In my opinion Sartre is reacting in a purely
sentimental way to this Israeli business (just as you are). But
what makes you conclude that I loathe Sartre? In the European
world there is no better current in the anti-imperialist struggle,
which remains the left's main objective and necessity, than the
'Sartrian' current. And Sartre's mistake (in my opinion) on
the Israeli issue doesn't affect that essential fact at all. I'm not
backtracking by writing these lines, mind you. But this idea of
yours that I 'loathe the non-Communist left' (if we may leave
aside Mollet) is completely absurd.

6. On the refugees — and this is important — despite your
entirely unwarranted analogy with the refugees in Germany,
despite the extremely hasty idea you put forward that they
could (and should?) have been settled in the neighbouring Arab

countries, which would of course have legitimated and sealed their dispossession, what I retain from your letter is that you seem to agree very clearly that they should be allowed to return to their land. I agree completely with making this, resettling them that is, one element of the solution — not the only element. See what I said above. But Israel has always said: out of the question.

7. You throw all sorts of reproaches at me about my errors, my asinities, my fanaticism, etc. etc. For my part I limit myself to observing that your positions are marred by a fundamental contradiction. On this point you do not manage to settle your thoughts clearly about what is or should be in the last analysis crucial: Israel's imperialist role or attitude. Let's not play with words: when an attitude is constant, the difference between an attitude and a role becomes less significant; and if the word 'role' means that Israel is a docile tool of imperialism, I'm not suggesting that and I don't believe that. Nor do I believe that the Israelis' role or attitude towards the Arabs can be identified with the South Africans'. I repeat: Israel is not the <u>main</u> cause of the oppression of the Arab masses, while the exploitation of the South African blacks etc.

About your contradictions: I've just reread your letter attentively, and I take it back. There is no contradiction in what you say — alas. I would prefer contradictions to the pure and simple denial that you end up with in your second letter of Israel's central or auxiliary, massive or slightly, imperialist role. When I say that it doesn't prevent the national or social emancipation of the Arab world but only fetters it, you say that 'I don't think that argument is worth much'. The idea that Israel is a threat to Arab liberation is 'preposterous', you say. In response to all this there's nothing at all I can say. There is no longer even room for dialogue. I cited Suez and the threat to Egypt; I cited the Israeli attitude (I was going to say role, but I corrected myself right away) in the Algerian business (but those Algerians have been such a disappointment to us,

haven't they?) and the Iraqi business. The presence of Israeli
paratroopers in the Congo in the good old days of Tshombe, a
major presence, major enough to ensure the training of anti-
rebel, pro-mercenary Congolese paratroopers. Nowadays they're
talking about Israeli paratroopers in Latin America, and not
fighting alongside the guerrillas. *Si non è vero…*[18] I remind you
that Israel has in practice protected the ungrateful Hussein. I
cite all these facts to you, and yet what you manage to respond
is, 'This [Israeli] imperialism consists, it seems to me [how nice
that you're not categorical about it], in wanting to defend its
borders against hostile neighbours.' So attacking the Congolese
rebels, attacking the <u>Algerian revolution</u>, is defending Israel's
borders. Protecting Hussein is defending Israel's borders. Here
your language is the language of the whole Israeli right.

When it isn't the language of the Israeli right — since I've found
a contradiction in your letter after all — is when you write: 'It
is in fact Israel's great historic misfortune, which may yet cost
it its existence, that no alliances were available to it outside the
imperialist camp.' Quite right. This is why Herzl negotiated
with the tsar, the sultan and the Kaiser. This is why the Zionist
movement negotiated with British imperialism. This is why all
these European Jews in the *belle époque* sought out only these
particular alliances, while despising, ignoring and denying the
existence of those wretched Palestinians. And why it keeps on
happening. Why they've never explored the possibility of an
understanding with the Arabs, except for a few noble minds,
except for a few intellectuals like Buber.[19]

I say and I repeat that if, as you admit, Israel couldn't have had
any alliances except imperialist ones, and if this is the way it's
always been, then we can speak of an imperialist state. While
you for your part conclude from Israel's foreign policy — not on

---

18   Italian saying: 'Even if it's not true, it's telling.'
19   Martin Buber (1878-1965), a Jewish philosopher and theologian born
      in Vienna, emigrated to Palestine in 1938 and worked to promote
      understanding between Jews and Arabs.

one point but on many points, and practically in light of Israel's
<u>whole</u> foreign policy, 'Speaking of Israel as an imperialist state
seems to me ... evidence of an extraordinary bias.'

To conclude, since there's no point to any of this, since we've
come to the point that we're accusing each other of being
biased (but good God, don't imagine that you're 'a good deal
more open-minded' than I). On 2 June 1967, you 'only hope[d]
that the Israelis wo[uld]n't do anything to make things worse,
even if this mean[t] their losing Eilat'. Today there's no longer
any room for doubt: they've gone for the jugular, as they'd
been threatening to do for two weeks. It seems to me that the
role of the left, of socialists, must be the following: completely
disregarding the question of whether individual socialists
are Jewish or not, to indicate (since we're not in a position to
demand or insist on anything at all) that any solution of the
Israeli-Arab conflict would require recognition on both sides of
the divide:

1) of the Israeli nation's right to exist (and I am deliberately not
using the formula 'the Israeli state');
2) of the need to rectify the injustice that has been done to the
Palestinian people.

But all the Jews, and everyone on the left who gives primary
if not exclusive attention in this tragic affair to one single
imperative (the two million Jews' right to exist), are partial and
only taking part of the problem into account. This is not enough
to convince the Arabs that they should do the same. But it's
more than enough to convince the Israelis — if they needed any
convincing — that what they're defending in the Middle East is
their existence, justice, law and civilization. Because Israel asks
for nothing more than this formula: its right to exist. It forgets
everything else. You can make whatever reproaches you want
about Israel's foreign or domestic policies, you can make all the
criticisms or express all the reservations you like, but as long as
you put forward only one decisive, clear, categorical conclusion
— that the Arabs must recognize Israel's right to exist; as long

as you don't add a second imperative — which I think I've made sufficiently clear — to this first one, whose corollary it is incidentally; as long as you restrict yourself (except for a few nuances and reservations) to <u>one</u> basic proposition, you're not bothering the people running Israel at all. They're not asking you for anything else. And we're giving it to them — well, except for me, and along with me some other members of the non-Communist left in Belgium and France, and some Communists too. [...]

Your friend,

Marcel

Draft letter (never sent)
[*Letterhead: London School of Economics and Political Science*]

16 June 1967

Dear Marcel,

My silence has been due to the fact that I've been thinking over our correspondence in light of the recent events, and been trying to judge to what extent they undermine my views and confirm yours. I had started to write to you two days after the war broke out, but I found that I was hesitating, and needed to question and re-examine what we were discussing. This is where I've gotten to:

1. Let's forget about Israel for a moment and look at things more broadly. For years now there has been a major movement of decolonization in the Arab world, which people like us need to support wholeheartedly. There was no question in my last letter of harbouring resentment towards you, God knows, for your support for the Algerians. The only thing is that the fact remains that the experience of these Arab liberation movements, important as they are, has very clear limits from a socialist point of view. This in no way detracts from the positive, anti-imperialist side (with its real limits) of these movements. What I was emphasizing, and what I still maintain, is that we tend to sugar-coat the pill and attribute <u>socialist</u> merits to these movements that they scarcely deserve. This is part of a weakness of judgment and lack of clarity that has also characterized the left's views on African 'socialist' decolonization movements. Let there be no misunderstanding here: this doesn't make me say that these movements aren't worthy of support, but rather

that we should support them in a socialist way, that is, see and even assert their limits. So to take a concrete example, it seems to me a positively bad thing that the left and USSR's support for Nasser's Egypt has made them keep quiet about the tortures that Egyptian Communists have been subjected to in Nasser's prisons. We have closed our eyes and kept our mouths shut too much about this kind of thing, about the limited character of the Nasserite experience, about Nkrumah's stupidities and faults and crimes in Ghana, just as the left did for the USSR in the good old days and just as it's still doing. In relation to the USSR, this attitude has been changing. But the same phenomenon is visible in the decolonizing countries.

2. This brings me to Israel. Two hypotheses: either Israel is a major factor holding back the anti-imperialist struggle — in that case the Arab attitude to Israel is justified; or it isn't, and only serves as an excuse for big manoeuvres meant to consolidate the Arab world, whose unity is fragile or mythical. Personally, I still think that it's the second hypothesis that's correct, and I even think this war, which I'll come back to later, confirms me in this opinion. In truth I don't see how Israel has been playing the imperialists' game in this war, or even how it <u>could</u> do so. At a certain point it seemed as if the Egyptian defeat would lead to Nasser's fall. But this was definitely not the case, and it seems quite likely to me that his resignation followed by his return, sealed by a plebiscite, were cleverly orchestrated. I'm glad it worked (Nasser's return, I mean), but I don't see any intention here to overthrow a progressive regime, to speak *in shorthand.* The same applies to the regime in Damascus. Everything you tell me about the Israelis' pro-Western attitudes is justified. But, to take up again a distinction that I think is useful, Israel's <u>role</u> in the application of imperialist pressure does not seem very substantial to me. I condemn its attitudes, but I don't see them as a serious obstacle to the development of the Arab anti-imperialist movement. You'll say that I'm blindly pro-Israeli. I have been questioning and examining myself, particularly since

the war, but I don't see it. Or at least, I don't see enough of it to make Israel a <u>major</u> trump card in the imperialist game.

3. The war. Here I'm frankly torn apart by contradictory considerations. On the one hand, the view that this preventive war (as they call it) doesn't solve anything *in the long run*, etc. But that's not the real question. What needs to be settled is not whether the war has solved anything, but whether it could be defended in principle, that is by considerations of survival etc., which I'll also come back to. One of two things must be true: either there was never any question of an Arab attack, in which case the war has been a monstrous crime; or there was a real possibility of one, in which case it could be justified or at least be open to discussion. Apparently Nasser didn't want a war, or didn't want it much; he was hesitating; he was warned not to attack, etc. The difficulty is that one can't really be certain about this. It's quite possible that the Egyptians wouldn't have made a move. But their occupation of the Gaza Strip, their mobilization, and the frenetic statements of many Arab leaders, including Nasser's statements to his air force officers, left a terrible doubt hanging in the air. I'm not speaking of Aqaba as a *casus belli*. A firm statement from Nasser without any circumlocution that there was no question of launching a war would have clarified things. But there were many statements that left doubts hanging in the air. And doubts meant for Israel, in the event of bad judgment on their part, a sentence to a massacre, or at least a campaign on Israeli territory without control of the air and in very difficult strategic circumstances. It's all very well for us to say that the Israelis should have *taken a chance,* hoped that nothing would happen, trusted in providence, etc. I feel I'm being very ambiguous here, incapable of saying that there was <u>no</u> justification for a preventive attack, and equally incapable of saying that there was <u>every</u> justification for this kind of attack. I don't doubt that it's easy to condemn this ambiguity. But I don't think the condemnation would take enough account of the real difficulties of the situation. I repeat: it's not enough to

cite Nasser's pacific statements, when he made other statements and gestures that left doubts hanging in the air, in circumstances where doubt signified terrible dangers. I emphasize this point. The possible attack could not have been repulsed at the frontiers, as would be the case in most countries. Given the geographical situation of the country, either the Israelis had to attack first or they were facing the prospect of vanishing from the face of the earth, or at least of a ferocious war on a scanty territory that in the best of cases would have left a wasteland of ruins in its wake. This was not the case for Egypt, or Syria, or even Jordan.

4. So let's suppose that the Israelis have attained a valid objective: warding off a direct military threat. There can be no question of accepting Dayan and others' vile declarations, or of accepting Israel's territorial claims. But neither can there be any question of going back to the status quo ante. That is, the state of Israel must be recognized, along with reabsorption of some of the refugees and compensation for the rest. This brings us back therefore to the previous discussion, in more difficult political conditions, but in a situation in which the survival of the state of Israel is no longer in question, at least for a long time to come. This means in my opinion that a socialist standpoint requires intransigent opposition to Israeli claims, an absolute condemnation of their treatment of the refugees, etc. But not acceptance of the Arab refusal to recognize their state.

5. This is precisely what I think you don't accept, and thus you find yourself beyond the Russian positions, beyond anybody's positions except those of the most nationalist Arab leaders. That's where I can't follow you at all.

Ralph

[*Letterhead: London School of Economics and Political Science*]

2 July 1967

Dear Marcel,

I'm very sorry not to have written to you sooner, but I've been very busy these last few weeks, and in any case I was thinking about recent events and trying to see how they affected my views on Israel etc. I do hope that you won't have misinterpreted my silence and attributed it to some kind of sulkiness.

Our discussion could only really be carried on in person, but I think I can identify the fundamental differences between us. The main one, which determines all the others, is Israel's existence or non-existence as a <u>state</u>. I read your manifesto in *La Gauche*[20] and think I can understand your references to the 'Israeli nation' whose right to existence you grant, no doubt in the framework of a Jewish-Arab or Arab-Jewish state. If that's really what your manifesto means (and it might have been good to clarify that point), then it seems to me something of a fantasy and even

---

20   The manifesto in question was entitled 'For a solution to the Israeli-Arab conflict', drafted mainly by Marcel Liebman, and signed by a long list of prominent individuals including 14 MPs and senators and many university faculty members. Dated 9 June 1967, it declares that 'the re-establishment of genuine peace in the Middle East will involve meeting two conditions, each of which is of *equal* importance: recognizing the Israeli nation's right to exist and discussing with its representatives the consequences that flow from that; and acknowledgement of the fact that the Arabs of Palestine are the victims of a profound injustice, to which the fate of over a million refugees bears witness, and of the necessity of repairing this injustice by granting them compensation and through the return to their country of those among them who wish to return.' *La Gauche* (Brussels), no. 24, 17 June 1967.

a refusal to deal with reality, rather than a way of solving the problems.

I'll explain briefly (I hope) what I mean: I shouldn't have to repeat, *but will do so all the same,* that personally I have no Zionist feeling at all, meaning that I don't see Israel as a 'solution' to the 'Jewish problem'; and I have no feeling for Israel itself, don't see it as a 'special' country, etc. Its existence has allowed some Jews who have been persecuted here and there to find refuge, but that's not a valid reason to preach the existence of the state of Israel, that is as a land of refuge for persecutions to come. I don't myself underestimate what that could mean for persecuted people, or Jews who fear persecution, or who are living in a hostile environment and in a country that seems hostile (the 'people's democracies', or some of them, alas), but, I repeat, this isn't a conclusive argument for supporting the right of an Israeli state to exist. What's conclusive is the fact of this state's existence. It was born in arbitrary conditions, by force, against the will of the neighbouring countries; but it didn't supplant any other existing state; and although I would have preferred the creation of a Jewish-Arab or Arab-Jewish state at the time, I've been forced to realize that everything — the history and evolution of the peoples in question, politics, sociology, etc. — made this solution entirely impossible and unacceptable for the forces on the ground. We can certainly discuss Israel's borders, the refugees, anything you like, but it seems impossible to me for us to seriously discuss the existence of this state, as a fact, which can only be changed by force, that is by the liquidation of the nation (in one way or another: expulsion and/or liquidation) as the practical result of the liquidation of the state. The two things are absolutely connected here. No doubt this shouldn't be the case, and won't be the case one day, but for the present and into the rather distant future it will be the case. Any present-day solution that doesn't take this fact into account must logically envisage the disappearance of this state by force — there is no other way to do it. The Russians etc. seem to rule out this solution when they speak of Israel's right to exist, while at the same time they seem to pay court to purely nationalist Arab tendencies. In this respect they show a certain lack of coherence, which incidentally Arab leaders like Nasser may also share in. The Chinese for their part seem to envisage Israel's disappearance in some way or another, which strikes me as coherent but unacceptable. Whatever the case, it is necessary to be clear and not leave any room for ambiguity on this basic given; and I'm afraid that your manifesto does leave room for ambiguity. The Arab leaders have done so as well, at least some of them have, and in my opinion this ambiguity has weakened their case considerably. If for example they had recognized the existence of an Israeli state, even with reservations about its exact frontiers and a fierce hostility to its policies, the Israelis would not have had the same audience that they got as a result of the Arab threats; and they would have found it much more difficult to [maintain] that the Israeli leaders, faced with the Arab actions and gestures of the previous weeks and the incendiary declarations on the official radio stations, found themselves in a terrible dilemma, which put in question or threatened to put in question Israel's national existence etc. It seems a bit frivolous to me to say that the Arab countries weren't <u>really</u> threatening Israel; it was impossible to be <u>completely</u> sure about Nasser's intentions; that is, his options were open. For the Israelis this constituted a big danger. And without the least enthusiasm, I can entertain the preventive argument.

That said, none of this forces me to endorse any aspect whatsoever of the Israeli claims, their conduct of the war, their attitude towards the refugees, or their policies in relation to anything. My acceptance of the Israeli national reality forces me to accept some conclusions about the country's right to defend itself, but absolutely nothing more. Take note that it is entirely possible to accept Israel's national reality and <u>condemn</u> Israeli aggression on this basis; both choices are possible, and

I chose one or the other option alternately during those two weeks, which means that the answer in my opinion is very far from being obvious. But I <u>start</u> by accepting the national reality. Everything else seems to me subject to serious discussion; what makes discussion virtually impossible and leads simply to the expression of two incompatible positions is the failure to accept this reality. This is what I thought I understood in reading and thinking about your letters and the manifesto. The refugees, reparations, foreign policy, etc., are all perfectly good subjects for serious discussion, but without touching on the heart of the problem. If you tell me that on the contrary these subjects, in particular the very presence of the state in Palestine, <u>prevent</u> acceptance of the Israeli reality, and that this reality as embodied in a state must be rejected before any other subject can be dealt with, then I can only take note of that opinion, state my disagreement with it, *and leave it at that.*

None of this resolves any of our differences, but I wanted at least to get back in touch and also make inquiries about your health. [...]

Your friend,

Ralph

[*Letterhead: Clos des Pommiers Fleuris*]

Brussels, 4 July 1967

Dear Ralph,

I was very happy to receive your letter after this interminable silence. I admit that I did in fact attribute it to a kind of 'sulkiness', although it seemed flabbergasting to me that this could be the result of a controversy that, while admittedly a bit lively, was all in all perfectly legitimate. Since the idea that you could have gone over to the camp of pro-Israeli or pro-Jewish patriotism seemed preposterous to me, I was reduced to not understanding anything at all… But enough of that.

I won't deal any more here with the heart of the problem. I do in fact think that an oral discussion would make more sense, that is if we could have it in a less impassioned way. Perhaps when we're both very old…. But at least one thing is comforting in this business: we haven't yet reached the age of wisdom. One remark just the same. To cite your words (curious how we've acquired a taste for citations — we're turning into genuine Marxist-Leninists): 'The refugees, reparations, foreign policy, etc., are all perfectly good subjects for serious discussion, but without touching on the heart of the problem. If you tell me that on the contrary these subjects, in particular the very presence of the state in Palestine, prevent acceptance of the Israeli reality, and that this reality as embodied in a state must be rejected before any other subject can be dealt with, then I can only take note of that opinion, state my disagreement with it, *and leave it at that.*'

That isn't my position. It isn't so much the existence of the state of Israel that prevents recognition of the Israeli nation or of the Israeli reality. It's the policies carried out by Israel (domestically — exclusion of non-Jews, treatment of the Arab minority — and internationally) — added to the weight of the past, to the wrongs that you mention ('born in arbitrary conditions, by force, against the will of the neighbouring countries...') — that can prevent this state's Arab neighbours from recognizing it. That's why, in a note I drafted for a press conference that was published in *La Gauche*, I think two weeks ago,[21] I spoke of recognition of Israel as the 'culmination' of a gradual détente (linked to a change in Israeli policies, but also — I agree — to greater realism on the Arabs' part, a realism that does not imply negotiations with and recognition of Israel at this point) and not as a precondition to this détente. There is no other solution; the alternative is a succession of Suezes.

[...]

Your friend,

Marcel

---

21 This was a press conference held in Brussels on 20 June 1967 in Brussels by the signers of the manifesto 'For a solution to the Israeli-Arab conflict' (see note 19 above). Marcel Liebman introduced the manifesto with a speech whose text was published in *La Gauche* no. 25 (24 June 1967). The text includes these words: 'Once the Arab grievances have been understood, it must be stated that they do not authorize putting in question the existence and survival of a nation of two million souls. Rejecting a situation that is felt to be profoundly unjust cannot go so far as envisaging an even more profound injustice. Having said this, if one considers the launching of a dialogue between Israel and the Arab states as an indispensable precondition for the establishment of genuine, lasting peace in the Middle East, doesn't it make sense to ask if it can be a precondition for such a dialogue that one side accept a condition that it has always rejected? Doesn't it seem more reasonable to think that this recognition of the state of Israel by the Arabs, after conflicts and struggles that are almost as old as this century, can only be the *culmination* of a process of détente and a labour of reconciliation that, according to all indications, will unfortunately take a very long time?'

...to a brotherly convergence
(by way of conclusion)

Gilbert Achcar

The two friends' positions on the Israeli-Arab conflict would continue to evolve for the rest of their lives, propelled by successive wars as well as by broader shifts in the *Zeitgeist*.

As we have seen in the preceding exchange of letters, their divergence quickly moved to its climax in the days just before the June 1967 war. The cathartic effect of the war at the same time set them moving back towards a convergence. After having gone so far as to defend Israel's foreign policy by looking for extenuating circumstances for it, Ralph Miliband became more and more critical of its behaviour.

The Six-Day War sealed a strategic alliance between the Zionist state and the United States, at a moment when the imperialist image of the US was at its worst due to its massive involvement in Vietnam. From this time on the US played the role of Israel's protector. In the Western radical left this caused a sharp falling off of the sympathy that a large number of people had felt for Israel, which Moscow had sponsored until not long before and which had enjoyed considerable credit on the left thanks both to memories of the Nazi genocide and to perceptions of the kibbutzim as advanced models of socialism. The Israeli invasion of Lebanon, almost 15 years to the day after the 1967 war (it began on 6 June 1982), completed the shift in the broader Western left's perception of Israel. The Palestinians' cause won correspondingly more support.

Ralph Miliband took part in this general shift:

He was deeply critical of many aspects of Israeli policy and from 1967 onwards was increasingly committed to the establishment of a Palestinian state. Nor was this his final position, as he ultimately become far more opposed to Israel, with a decisive change in attitude following its invasion of the Lebanon in June 1982.[1]

As the years passed, therefore, Ralph moved steadily closer to his friend Marcel Liebman's harsh attitude towards the state of Israel. He came to see through the illusions that he had had before the June 1967 war about this state's function in the world imperialist order, and no longer worried about its short- or middle-term survival now that Israel with US backing was maintaining a crushing military superiority over all its neighbours put together. Nevertheless Ralph remained committed to the idea of the necessity of the Arabs' recognizing the Israeli 'national reality [...] as embodied in a state'.

The only programme for a solution to the Israeli-Palestinian conflict that would be at all equitable, while being both reasonable and realistic, in his eyes, was the coexistence of two states, one Israeli and one Palestinian. On this point he had the satisfaction of seeing his friend Marcel move towards this same position, as in fact most of the Palestinian movement did as well.

The 'Two-State' Solution

In his letter of 4 July 1967, the last one included in this collection, Marcel accepted Ralph's perspective of Arab recognition of the state of Israel, which he had already endorsed in his press conference on 20 June 1967, as the 'culmination' of a shift in the two sides' attitudes.

Nonetheless, he remained torn between this position and the position of Fatah,[2] the predominant organization of Israel's Palestinian victims. Fatah's official ideology, or at least the version

---

1   Michael Newman, *Ralph Miliband and the Politics of the New Left*, London: Merlin Press, 2002, p. 135.
2   The organization founded and led by Yassir Arafat.

of its ideology intended for export, called for replacing the 'Jewish' state of Israel with a 'democratic and secular' state of Palestine on the whole of the territory that had previously fallen under the British colonial Mandate. Out of internationalist generosity and with much optimism, Marcel initially confused the Fatah formula with the formula of a 'binational' state.[3]

In fact this famous formula deliberately used the characterization 'secular' – simply addressing the issue of a multireligious state. In 1969, the year in which the formula was put forward, Fatah, like the whole of the Arab national or nationalist movement, refused to recognize the existence of an *Israeli* national reality, and relegated the Israelis to the status of *Jewish* inhabitants of the occupied Palestinian territory. The formula was intended to transform Israeli Jews from a population of colonists into a religious community enjoying equal rights within a democratic Palestinian state. In this period Yasser Arafat liked to cite Lebanon as a model of democratic coexistence among different communities.

The Palestinian writer Elias Sanbar, editor of the *Revue d'Etudes Palestiniennes*, has contributed his recollection, quite sincerely, of the origin of the idea of a 'democratic secular state' in Palestine: the idea was born in response to pressure from Fatah's friends abroad, who reproached it with not having any programme for the future of a liberated Palestine.

> So, and this was the root of it all, the idea was to respond to these reproaches, to earn our 'passport' and achieve the status of a revolutionary movement, and to get rid of the characterization, which was pejorative at the time, as a 'nationalist' movement. This is why the leadership of the resistance, already equipped with an impressive degree of pragmatism, asked a little group of intellectuals among its members, professors in fact at the American University of Beirut, to write a coherent text. The group

3 'What the Palestinians ask for today is the end of Israel [...] and its replacement with a "secular democratic", that is, binational Palestine.' Marcel Liebman, 'Nouvelles perspectives?', *Mai* (Brussels), March 1969, p. 42.

– coordinated by Nabil Shaath, now a minister in the Palestinian
Authority – went on to publish a long article in 1969 *in English* –
evidence that the work was aimed first of all at a foreign audience
– in the semi-underground journal *Fatah,* which the movement's
Information Department was then publishing in Beirut. Somewhat
later the Fatah cell in Paris, which I belonged to, took on the task
of spreading the French translation of the text. […]
Thus we see that this founding text on the future of the Palestinians
and Israelis was never published in Arabic, the language of those
it primarily addressed. On the contrary, perceived as a weapon in
the struggle, it was aimed at the outside world, in order to show it
in a way that the Palestinian movement, so often belittled, had its
own original 'theoretical reflection'; in order to reduce to silence
all those who were accusing the Palestinians of wanting to drive
the Jews into the sea; and equally to reassure the friends who were
constantly asking, 'What will you do with the Jews if you liberate
your country?'[4]

Marcel Liebman was one of these friends, and his friendship
had even led him to read a content into the formula that it
definitely did not have. But it did not take him long to realize it.
In the long essay that he wrote in 1970 at Ralph's request for the
Socialist Register, the yearbook that Ralph Miliband had founded
and edited, Marcel cited this same formula again, but this time
taking some distance from it. He had rightly understood that the
formula, by ignoring the 'Israeli national reality', could not truly
convince the Israelis. He had become aware of the importance of
a feeling of danger for the consolidation of Zionist ideology:

It is vain and absurd to call upon a nation to renounce a state
machine, juridical structures and a policy of hegemony, even
though these be indefensible from the standpoint of democratic
(and *a fortiori* socialist) principles, if the nation thinks that this
state, these structures and this mistaken and agonizing will to
hegemony are the conditions necessary for its survival.[5]

4   Elias Sanbar, 'Post-scriptum', Michel Warschawski, *Israël-Palestine: le défi
     binational,* Paris: Textuel, 2001, pp. 137-38.
5   Liebman, 'Israel, Palestine and Zionism', *The Socialist Register,* London,
     1970, p. 106.

He called on the left to make 'more precise, in alliance with the Arab Left, the formula of a bi-national Palestine, in conformity with the needs of its existing population, which at present is recognized only by the Democratic Popular Front for the Liberation of Palestine.'[6]

As a matter of fact, the DPFLP had for a time timidly put forward the programmatic perspective of a binational (socialist) state in Palestine, citing Yugoslavia as a model. This perspective was soon forgotten, however. It later made a vigorous comeback in a completely different context: the failure of the Oslo process begun in 1993 and the increasingly interwoven presence of Israeli and Palestinian inhabitants due to Israeli settlement on the West Bank.[7]

Meanwhile, the October 1973 war — which the Israelis call the Yom Kippur War and the Arabs call the Ramadan War — sped up the shifts in the official Arab programme of demands in general, and of the Fatah-dominated Palestinian 'centre', the PLO, in particular.[8] The time had come to demand a Palestinian state alongside Israel — even if the assumption of a (necessarily peaceful) coexistence of two states remained implicit in the initial period.

Ralph nonetheless did not fail to rejoice at this development in a letter to Marcel:

---

6 Ibid., p. 108. The DPFLP (Democratic Popular Front for the Liberation of Palestine, led by Nayef Hawatmeh, later the DFLP) had left the PFLP (Popular Front for the Liberation of Palestine, led by George Habash) in 1969, claiming a revolutionary Marxist orientation.

7 For recent debates on the 'binational' formula, see Gary Sussman, 'The Challenge to the Two-State Solution', *Middle East Report*, Washington, no. 231, Summer 2004. For a critique of the formula, see Salim Tamari, 'The Dubious Lure of Binationalism', *Journal of Palestine Studies*, Washington-Berkeley, vol. 30, no. 1, Autumn 2000.

8 On this phase of the PLO's evolution, I take the liberty of referring to my own analyses, published in Gilbert Achcar, *Eastern Cauldron*, New York: Monthly Review Press, 2004.

I must say that things in the Middle East seem to me to be headed in the right direction — that is that everybody, all at once, seems, with more or less reservations, to accept the idea that I've always subscribed to myself, that is creating a Palestinian state alongside Israel, if possible including Jordan, or else not including Jordan; *but anyway a state*, an institutional foundation, on the basis of which more could be built *in time to come*, hypothetically with federalism, etc. etc. In my opinion there is no other possibility and never has been; and it seems that finally, thanks to the oil blackmail carried out by those foul Arab regimes, that the pressure on Israel will be sufficient to bring it to the negotiating table. No doubt this isn't the 'revolutionary' solution, or rather it isn't the solution that the extremist supporters of a secular democratic state foresaw, but that solution never was a solution, *at the present time and for a long time to come*; whereas my solution is possible, puts the Palestinians back in the historical and geographical swing of things and opens up new vistas.[9]

Marcel for his part moved in the same direction. In 1980 he published an article containing an implicit but nonetheless drastic revision of one aspect of his post-1967 standpoint. He welcomed the fact that a 'very real softening has taken place in the Palestinians' positions', which now accepted 'coexistence with Israel' as a 'sufficient objective, at the very least as a transitional step towards a unitary Palestine'.[10] He even went so far as declaring that European governments 'should bring the PLO to understand that no peace will be possible in the Middle East if the Israelis' desire to keep their state is not taken into account'. 'Declaring or suggesting, in supposedly revolutionary rhetoric, that the PLO's objective is the elimination of Israel will only make Israelis cling more firmly to an intransigence that is all too much in keeping with their consistent practice.'[11]

Ralph expressed great satisfaction at this final step in the two

---

9   Miliband to Liebman, 23 November 1973, Marcel Liebman Foundation collection, Free University of Brussels [passages in italics in English in the original].

10   Liebman, 'L'an trente-trois du conflit israélo-arabe', *La Revue Nouvelle* (Brussels), no. 10, 1980, p. 304.

11   Ibid., p. 308.

friends' convergence. 'I very much liked your article, which seems to me quite correct.' Except for a slight shade of difference, he could now write, 'I am very happy to see that we are very close to one another on the fundamentals.'[12]

Marcel Liebman travelled to Israel for the first time in 1982. This visit finished the process of confirming him in his new conviction that no settlement advantageous to the Palestinian people would be possible without taking account of the fear that bound Israeli society together in a stance of Zionist intransigence — the same fear that he had previously refused to take seriously.

> On one point, my pre-existing schema has burst apart. I had always been convinced that the security argument that surfaces so often in the Israeli discourse was a propaganda trick and a form of blackmail meant for foreign consumption. It seemed unthinkable to me that the Israelis really felt fear in face of the Palestinian or even Arab 'threat'. This is a people that has triumphed military in each of the Middle East's wars, and most often won overwhelming victories. This people has one of the world's strongest armies, whose effectiveness forms a singular contrast with the individual and collective weakness of the Arab armies. [...]
>
> And yet in the heart of this Israeli people lies fear. [...] There is a whole set of explanations for this phenomenon. Without wanting to peer into the depths of the nation's soul, clearly the history of persecution experienced by the Jews of Europe plays a major, fundamental role in this anxiety. To this I would also add that the Israeli state and Jewish community leaders around the world have always busied themselves not in healing these wounds, which in any case heal only with difficulty, but in keeping them festering. They find a justification in the Nazi genocide for certain policies (the intransigence of the contemporary Jew who refuses to be a victim any more).
>
> But closer to home there are the lasting effects brought about by the Palestinians' recourse to violence and terror. The PLO attacks, which up until 1975 targeted the Israeli civilian population, have left deep scars in Israelis' collective consciousness. I make no moral judgment here of the recourse to terrorism. National liberation movements have made it a classic weapon, which

---

12   Miliband to Liebman, 22 October 1980.

expresses both the radicalism of their demands and the weakness of their resources. I only note that the PLO's activities in their terrorist phase went hand in hand with its consolidation and reinforcement, but also at the same time with the avowed hatred of the vast majority of Israelis for Palestinian nationalists. [...] To this we must add that the Israeli state — both the Likud government and Labour opposition — reinforces this image; that the right indulges in this field in constant, boundless demagogy (Arafat = Hitler, any negotiation with the PLO = a new Munich!), and that Peres' social democrats do not have the courage to come out clearly in opposition to this demagogy, so that they always seem to be tagging along behind their chauvinist rivals.

Still, this deep anxiety of the Israelis has to be taken into account.[13]

Not long after these lines were written, on 10 April 1983, Issam Sartawi, the Palestinian negotiator who at that time had gone the furthest in engaging in dialogue with Israelis with the aim of reaching a peaceful settlement of the conflict between the two peoples, was assassinated by a killer belonging to Abu Nidal's terrorist group. Marcel Liebman wrote indignantly,

Yet neither the Israelis nor the Palestinians will find the way to compromise and reconciliation if the world continues to close its ears to the undeniable truths that Sartawi never tired of repeating: peace is impossible unless the Palestinians, like all the world's other peoples, are granted the right to self-determination; it is just as indispensable for the Arabs to accept Israel's right to exist; failing this, the Middle East will remain a bear-garden and the Palestinian people will remain an uprooted, humiliated and consequently rebellious nation.[14]

The following year Liebman worded his prophetic warning even more clearly in the magazine of the Belgian-Palestinian Association:

Recognizing the Palestinian people's national rights and

---

13   Liebman, 'Retour d'Israël', *La Revue Nouvelle*, no. 2, 1983, p. 172-73.
14   Liebman, 'Sur la tombe de Sartaoui', *Le Soir* (Brussels), 11 April 1983.

advocating the concrete exercise of these rights is not incompatible with the Israeli people's interests. The true security to which this people aspires is linked to the creation of a Palestinian state, the indispensable precondition for the disappearance of the tensions, conflicts and wars that have been tearing the region apart for so long. If by contrast the Palestinians remain a people without a country, none of the inhabitants of the Middle East — including Israel's Jews — will escape from the impasse they find themselves in, with the cycle of terror and counter-terror that is its inevitable consequence.[15]

On 2 March 1986 Marcel Liebman died, after waging a long, painful battle, his last, against illness.[16] Ralph Miliband — for whom the Middle East conflict was always a relatively secondary concern and who only very rarely discussed the subject, except in his correspondence and in particular his exchanges with Marcel — did not try to take his friend's place in this area of Marcel's special interest. His biographer does, however, cite one last letter on the Israeli-Palestinian question, written to Edward Said on 17 November 1993, in which Miliband supported Said's opposition to the Oslo accords, considering them too favourable to Israel.[17]

In taking up this last position, Ralph stayed true to the memory of his best friend Marcel, to Marcel's unshakable attachment to the Palestinian people's rights, and to Marcel's conviction that there will be no peace without genuine recognition of the Palestinians' right to self-determination on an equal and reciprocal footing.

22 June 2005

---

15   Liebman, 'Pourquoi la Palestine ?', *Palestine* (Brussels), September 1984.
16   See the poignant text that he wrote about this last battle during the 'frightful night' of 1-2 July 1985 when he tried to tame death — published in *Marcel Liebman*, special issue of *Points Critiques*, quarterly journal of the Union of Progressive Jews of Belgium (Brussels), no. 25, May 1986.
17   Newman, op. cit., p. 163, note 77.

THE "SIX-DAY WAR": A CHRONOLOGY

PRELUDES

October-November 1956
Tripartite aggression – Israel, France and the U.K. – against Egypt, following the nationalisation of the Suez Canal by the regime of President Gamal Abdul Nasser.

February 1957
Deployment of the United Nations Emergency Force on the demarcation line between Egypt and Israel – on the Egyptian side only, as Israel refused to allow it to be stationed on the territory under its control. Accordingly, it was understood that the UNEF could be withdrawn at the request of the Egyptian government.

January 1964
Meeting in Cairo of the first summit of Arab heads of state. Creation of the Palestine Liberation Organisation (PLO).

January 1965
First operations by the military wing of the Palestinian organisation al-Fatah.

February 1966
The left-wing faction of the Syrian Ba'ath Party seizes power. Washington sees it as an equivalent of Castro's regime in Cuba.

May-August 1966
Repression of al-Fatah in Syria. Yasir Arafat is released after a hunger strike.
Repression of all Palestinian organisations in Jordan.

November 1966
Defence agreement between Syria and Egypt. Israeli reprisal raid against As-Samu, a Palestinian village under Jordanian jurisdiction (on the West Bank).

THE THIRD ARAB-ISRAELI WAR

8 April 1967
Following border incidents between the two countries, Israeli air raid on Syria: six Syrian airplanes shot down.

11-13 May 1967
Israeli threats against Syria. Moscow informs Egypt that Israel is massing troops on the Syrian border.

16-18 May 1967
Egypt requests the withdrawal of the UN force from its territory.

22 May 1967
Nasser announces the denial of access to the Gulf of Aqaba, and therefore to the Israeli port of Eilat, to Israeli ships and "strategic" shipments to Israel.

30 May 1967
Defence agreement between Jordan and Egypt.

1st June 1967
National Unity Government in Israel, bringing together the Labourites and the components of the future Likud Party.

5 June 1967
Israeli air force destroys the Egyptian air force on the ground by a surprise air raid at dawn.

5-10 June 1967
"Six-Day War": Israel seizes the rest of Palestine up to the Jordan River (the West Bank annexed by Jordan since 1949), the Gaza Strip (under Egyptian administration since 1949), the whole of the Egyptian Sinai Peninsula up to the Suez Canal and the Syrian Golan Heights.

Also available from The Merlin Press

MARXISM AND POLITICS

by Ralph Miliband

What is class conflict?
How do ruling classes and the state reproduce capitalism?
What is the role of the Party and what are the differences between reform and revolution?
This is a readable and engaging survey: mainly of key Marxist texts – Marx, Engels and Lenin – and of Marxist political experience. Miliband believes in a socialism which defend freedoms already won: and to make possible their extension and enlargement by the removal of class boundaries.

Reviews of the previous edition:

'This is probably the best introduction to Marx's Politics currently available and is as non-sectarian as the subject allows.' *Teaching Politics*

'A job excellently done...' *New Society*.

'The best primer on Marxism and politics ever written and Miliband's best book.' Leo Panitch: Professor of Politics, York University, Toronto

216 x 138 mm. viii, 200 pp.
ISBN. 0850365317
2004 paperback

RALPH MILIBAND AND THE POLITICS OF THE NEW LEFT

by Michael Newman

Based on exclusive access to Miliband's extensive personal papers, and supplemented by interviews, this book analyses the ideas and contribution of a key figure in the British and international Left from the second world war until the collapse of communism. Miliband's life and work form the central focus, but the book also provides an interpretative history of the evolution, debates and dilemmas of socialists throughout the period, and of the problems they faced both at work defending academic freedom and in society at large.

'Comprehensive, scholarly, sensitive and readable...one of the kindest men and the best minds in our generation.' From the foreword by Tony Benn.

'Admirably clear in its construction and scrupulously researched…Miliband's own interventions in his time live on…in his books and essays…but his personal writings, amply extracted here, give a vivid sense of the man behind them – making this a good book to have.' *New Left Review*.

'Not just a biography of one of the great socialist minds of the 20th century, it is the history of an entire period of leftist activity, buffeted as it was by WWII, Vietnam and the decline of the Communist bloc…as full and incisive a biography as he could have wished.' *Red Pepper*.

'An impeccably researched biography.' *Socialist History*.

234 x 156 mm. xiv, 368 pp.
ISBN. 0850365139
2nd impression with corrections, 2004 Paperback
Rights: USA - Monthly Review Press
Canada - Fernwood Puiblishing

LENINISM UNDER LENIN

by Marcel Liebman

This book, a winner of the Isaac Deutscher Memorial Prize, is an antidote to the view that Stalinism is synonymous with Leninism. Liebmann highlights democratic dimensions in Lenin's thinking as it developed over 25 years.

'I have not come across anything which captures so well the complexities of Lenin's positions.' Ralph Miliband.

'The author of this historical study of Lenin's political activities and theories combines a sympathetic understanding of Lenin's positions with a critical approach making it one of the most informative books on Lenin that have been written.' *Labour Research*.

214 x 134 mm. 477pp
ISBN. 085036261X
1975/1980 Paperback

Order these and other Merlin Press titles on line at:

www.merlinpress.co.uk